Angels and Demons

Angels and Demons

A Christian Primer of the Spiritual World

Michael Patella, OSB

LITURGICAL PRESS
Collegeville, Minnesota

www.litpress.org

1   2   3   4   5   6   7   8   9

Library of Congress Cataloging-in-Publication Data

Patella, Michael, 1954–
    Angels and demons : a Christian primer of the spiritual world / Michael Patella.
        p.   cm.
    Includes bibliographical references and index.
    ISBN 978-0-8146-3277-2 — ISBN 978-0-8146-3448-6 (e-book)
        1. Spirits.   2. Angels—Christianity.   3. Demonology.   4. Bible—Criticism, interpretation, etc.   I. Title.

BT963.P38 2012
235—dc23
                                                    2012008471

To the next generation,
Aaron, Beth, Kiri, and Meg,
as you engage the world seen and unseen

Contents

Preface   ix

Acknowledgments   xiii

Introduction   xv

PART 1
Sacred Scripture

Chapter 1: Pentateuch and Historical Books   3

Chapter 2: Wisdom Books   18

Chapter 3: Isaiah the Prophet   25

Chapter 4: New Testament   29

Conclusion   55

PART 2
Angels

Chapter 5: Development of Angels in the
          Christian Tradition   59

Chapter 6: Angels and Christ's Ministry: A Theology   71

Chapter 7: Souls: Immortality or Eternal Life?   80

Conclusion   103

PART 3
The Diabolical World

Chapter 8: Satan, the Devil, and Lucifer   107

Chapter 9: Dealing with the Devil   122

Chapter 10: The Occult   127

Chapter 11: Satan's Activities   134

Chapter 12: Neo-paganism   147

Conclusion   161

Notes   163

Bibliography   174

Further Reading   177

Scripture Index   179

Preface

The popular media are filled with books, movies, videos, and internet links on angels, demons, and the spiritual world in general. Highly entertaining for a great many people, these accounts vary in levels of accuracy in their presentation of Christianity. Instead of origin, aim, and purpose of the faith, the media mine Christianity for its props and do so without concern for its context or message. The cross is used to deflect a vampire, candles are lit in front of statues, or a priest is called to shout Latin incantations at the possessed. The deeper questions of what makes the cross sacred, why statues call people to prayer, or how a priest becomes the agent of exorcism are rarely discussed. Moreover, if these questions are addressed, the result can often be inaccurate to the point of making Christianity appear as mere superstition.

I have been teaching for most of my adult life, first in high school and now as a university professor. During the course of these years, my students both in class and privately have posed to me various and innumerable questions on issues dealing with life, death, Christ, Satan, and the Church as well as the occult. In response, I have had to face the hurdle of the sound bite, which our society has come to rely on to supply answers to even its most complicated questions. People expect ready and concise statements to their queries, but such answers, especially those addressing the spiritual world, are comprehensible only when we know the background, the context, and the grand narrative of the Christian Tradition.

This book is an attempt to construct as succinctly as possible the general framework into which the Christian understanding of the spiritual world exists. To do so, it draws on Christian Tradition as transmitted primarily through Sacred Scripture but also through liturgy and the Creed. It does not address every facet of the Christian life, for no work can do that, but through references and a bibliography, I hope that readers can pursue related topics on their own.

The book is divided into three major sections. Part 1 is general exegesis of both the Old and New Testaments and their treatment of angels, demons, and the spiritual world in general. It also elaborates on eschatology, or the end times, a major Christian theme in the Bible. Part 2 functions as an overview of the angelic realm and, by necessity, includes a discussion on souls, social justice, purgatory, and eternal life. Part 3 addresses the diabolical world, specifically Satan, Lucifer, and the devil, and discusses the development of our Christian understanding of evil spirits by tracing its history through the Pseudepigrapha and literary classics. It also presents an extended treatment of the occult, exorcism, neo-paganism, and even a feast day much discussed in certain circles, Halloween. In addition to the bibliography, I have supplied a short list of other, related works that may be of interest to readers.

This monograph is intended to be, as the title states, a Christian primer of the spiritual world. It is not an interfaith discourse on angels and demons. I write as a Catholic drawing upon the Christian Tradition, and I do so primarily for other Christians. I do not pretend to write on how other faiths view and deal with the realm of spirits. I am an outsider to all other faiths but my own, and as an outsider, I would be forced to presume a position of knowledge and authority that is not mine and to risk presenting the tenets of another religion inaccurately and unfairly. While there is some overlap of the subject matter with other religious traditions, I deal with them only insofar as they impact the Christian view or share with Christianity a line of development, particularly the two other Abrahamic faiths, i.e., Islam and especially Judaism.

My hope in this undertaking is that readers will arrive at a better understanding of how the spiritual world, a world integral to Christian belief, cannot be divorced from the faith revealed through the incarnation, ministry, death, and resurrection of Christ and the outpouring of his Holy Spirit upon the cosmos.

Acknowledgments

Many people have helped me in bringing this book to completion. I would like to thank Peter Dwyer, director of Liturgical Press, who first approached me about writing on angels and demons. His initial interest contributed a great deal to my own enthusiasm in composing this work. Also at the Liturgical Press, I would like to thank Hans Christoffersen, publisher; Ann Blattner, cover artist; Lauren L. Murphy, managing editor; and Barry Hudock, associate publisher.

I am most grateful to Nick Ratkay, Angela G. Del Greco, and Justin Taylor, SM, for their probing insights, comments, and suggestions for the piece and to Ursula Klie for her fine eye in proofreading the book's final draft. Finally, I would like to thank all my students over the course of the past seventeen years, whose questions, comments, concerns, and curiosity have been particularly responsible for demonstrating how pertinent the topic of angels, demons, and the spiritual realm are for the world today.

Introduction

Christ yesterday and today
the Beginning and the End
the Alpha
and the Omega
All time belongs to him
and all the ages
To him be glory and power
through every age and for ever. Amen.[1]

Any work which purports to present an explanation of angels
and demons, good and evil, or seen and unseen phenomena
runs the risk of falling into a dualistic view of the universe.
Despite strong arguments against such a stance, we are all prone
to divide the cosmos into two equal and opposing forces with
God, angels, and saints arrayed on the side of good, holding at
bay Satan, devils, and wicked souls, who themselves are forward-
ing all that is evil. This dualistic outlook forces us into conclud-
ing that we really do not know who will be victorious in the
grand battle at the end of time; we mortals can only hope that
we have not cooperated with the Evil One to such a degree as
to ostracize us from aligning with God and his good forces.

I would like to state at the outset of this book, therefore, that
the position I describe above, that is, the dualistic notion of

good and evil equally opposed in an eternal battle with each other, a battle whose final outcome is in doubt, is not the Christian view of creation. Indeed, it is the most un-Christian of all interpretations. It is an understanding that is not supported by either Scripture or Tradition.

The Christian faith rests on the unshakeable and irrefutable fact that our lives, as with all creation, are an integral part of Christ's own victory over sin and death, made so by his incarnation, passion, death, and resurrection. Christ has claimed creation for the forces of good, and the forces of evil are powerless to overcome them. Good has already won the battle, evil is on the run, and there is no chance of the tide ever turning the other way, evil actions and human suffering notwithstanding.

What I wish to address in the following pages is how Christianity, relying on its Scriptures, sacraments, and living Tradition deals with what is commonly called the "paranormal." This attempt is not a denial of either good or bad supernatural entities. Angels, souls, spirits, and demons exist, and although psychological conditions can easily be mistaken for them, the paranormal is not solely a psychological phenomenon.

PART 1

Sacred Scripture

Chapter 1

Pentateuch and Historical Books

Within the Christian Tradition, Sacred Scripture not only relates the narrative of salvation history but also occupies a sacramental position. Both the Old and New Testaments are the Word of God in human words.[1] The foundation of the Christian faith rests on the belief that this Word of God became flesh in the person Jesus Christ, a fact that Christians call the incarnation. Consequently, by reading the Bible, we not only see and hear the stories of God engaging his creation and his people but also hold in our hands the very grace and promise that has become incarnate in the person of Jesus Christ. To understand the role angels play in our lives and why demons interfere with us, we must ground all discussion on the implications of the incarnation. To do this, we must investigate the Bible itself, for it provides us with the storyline of God's dwelling among us.

The Pentateuch

Genesis

The story of the fall in Genesis 3:1-8 has become so familiar. Often our imagination has filled in details that the text does not supply. For instance, nowhere does it say that the serpent is the devil or is in league with him; yet, we all assume that Satan plays a role in the temptation of Adam and Eve. Genesis does not support such a conclusion, however. Even as Genesis continues on to the first murder by Cain of Abel, there is no mention of Satan. Nonetheless, God personifies sin in his warning to Cain: "sin is lurking at the door; its desire is for you, but you must master it" (Gen 4:7).

This reference provides us with two interesting trajectories with regard to evil and human complicity with that evil. First, sin or wrongdoing is not regarded as an act of a beneficent God; second, sin is equated with a malevolent being or demon whom the human being, Cain, can master. Still, there is no counter-force opposing God; a demon may run interference with the well-ordered universe, but in no way can this demon overpower either God or Cain. Cain's fault lies in granting that "lurking" sin authority over his human thoughts and actions.

Although nothing in Genesis 3 states that the serpent is the devil or Satan, the tempting, seductive tone of the conversation with Eve has most certainly set this reptile in league with the Evil One, if not identified it with him. There is nothing overtly wrong with our tendency to do so, but the association should alert us to the fact that in the biblical narrative, the identification of certain actions to Satan as well as defining Satan as a real supernatural being has a long line of development, and much of that development comes from sources outside the canonical text.

BENEVOLENT SPIRITS OR ANGELS

Genesis is much more expressive in dealing with angels than with demons. In the very story of the Fall, for example, once Adam and Eve are cast out from the Garden of Eden, the Lord God stations the cherubim at the entrance of the Garden to guard it. These great winged creatures do not threaten or even speak to the couple; they are solely in service to God, protecting all that is holy.[2] The next citation of an angel occurs in Genesis 16:7. Sarai's slave girl, Hagar, flees the maltreatment of her mistress, and an "angel of God" comes to rescue and console her.

Angels take on a major role in Genesis 18–19. Three angels, disguised as three traveling strangers, stop at the tent of Sarah and Abraham and are welcomed as guests.[3] The three live up to their name of "messenger," for the term "angel" is the English form of the Greek word *angelos*, a translation of the Hebrew *malachah*, which is used in this Genesis text and whose meaning is "messenger." Abraham and Sarah treat the supernatural beings according to the ancient code of hospitality. These three angels depart but not before leaving a blessing: they predict the birth of Isaac (Gen 18:10).

These three angels continue their journey to Sodom and Gomorrah (Gen 19:1-22). Actually, only two proceed to the notorious cities; one, who actually happens to be the Lord, stays back to inform Abraham of the impending disaster, and Abraham bargains with him to save the city. Alas, these angels can only rescue Lot and his family, so heinous is the sin of rape.[4]

The biblical narrative provides a valuable insight in this passage. It is not always clear in the Bible when the Lord is speaking and acting and when an angel is doing so as the Lord's agent. This confusion between the two underscores the closeness angels have with God; they represent their master very well. No matter how difficult a message may be, or even how unsettling or fearful an angelic visitation may seem, angels always bring goodness and blessing to either an individual or a company of people, if they heed the angelic message.[5] This characteristic is one distinguishing factor between demons and angels. Angels are good; demons are bad.[6]

Exodus

Just as Genesis shows an angel identified with God, so does Exodus with the theophany at the burning bush. The text states that "the angel of the Lord" appears to Moses (Exod 3:2), but the Lord himself calls out to Moses (3:4). Further on, the same kind of connection occurs between the Lord and the angel, recognized as a pillar of cloud by day and fire by night. This angel guards the people and leads them out from Egypt and into the Promised Land (Exod 13:21-22; 14:19, 24).

The writer of the Exodus goes to great lengths to show that Pharaoh has plenty of opportunities to cooperate with the Lord's plan for his people, as explicated by Moses; the Pharaoh, however, does not. The text has two explanations for the Pharaoh's stubbornness. The first is that Pharaoh hardens his heart, and the second is that the Lord hardens Pharaoh's heart. This account might sound grossly unfair or, at best, confusing. The purpose of the narrative is not to provide a smooth plot line; rather, it is to show the omnipotence of the Lord God and his abiding concern for his people. The Egyptians believed that Pharaoh controlled the social and natural worlds; Exodus wants to show that the Lord God and not Pharaoh is in charge of the universe, even if that makes the story line confusing.

Leviticus, Numbers, Deuteronomy

Throughout most of the Pentateuch, other than the references cited above, there are no other citations referring to demons, the devil, or Satan. Nonetheless, there are allusions and a basic understanding that anything that is not from the Lord is evil. The first commandment is a prohibition against idolatry, and reminders to avoid such practices surface throughout the remaining three books, particularly in Deuteronomy 4, 12, and 13. Although there are no explicit references to diabolical entities in these prohibitions, there arises from them the understanding that running after false gods is an abominable evil. We will return to this concept below, but suffice to say at this point that to the Lord belongs the earth and everything in it. To worship someone or something else, therefore, is to deny this fact, and the grievousness of such practices on the behalf of the Israelites is aggravated by the special, loving relationship the Lord has with the people he has chosen.

Idolatry is participating in a lie and falsehood. The Pentateuch may not acknowledge outright that other supernatural beings exist independently of the Lord, but it does not deny their presence in the world either. From the point of view of the various writers of these first five books of the Bible, the other gods are liars, imposters, pretenders, and to turn to them in worship is forsaking and insulting the one holy and true God.

Historical Books

Angels are prominent within the historical books doing what they do best: acting as messengers from God to his people. An angel gives Joshua the battle plan for Jericho (Josh 5:13–6:5). In the book of Judges, angels appear frequently, and not always with a friendly or positive message. The angel of the Lord who went up to Bochim upbraids the Israelites for making pacts with the native people in the Promised Land (Judg 2:1-3). Because of this transgression, the angel states that the inhabitants will not be cleared from the land and that their gods will become a "snare" for the Israelites. As the various episodes in Judges unfold, we can see that the pagan gods do not actively work against the Israelites—indeed, they are pretty passive. Rather, because God's people run to them instead of the Lord, they exchange a true and loving relationship for a false one, and when they do, their society faces difficult consequences. The Israelites then repent and return to the Lord only to apostatize yet again. It is a cycle that repeats itself over and over. Although the false gods are not equated with demons themselves, since they are false, nothing good can come from them, and nothing does.[7]

At this point in the OT narrative, the false gods are named: Baal and his consort, *Astarte(s)*.[8] Baal was the principal god of the Canaanites, Philistines, and Phoenicians surrounding the people Israel. Sometimes spelled *Bel* when compounded with another word, e.g., *Zerubbabel*, the word literally means "lord." It often appears in the plural form, and when it does, it means "gods." So, within this system, there would be one chief god, Baal, who was generally the storm god, as well as lesser baals, or gods, each with other spheres of influence, such as streams, forests, etc. It should be evident from the name how heinous it would be for the Israelites to run after the baals. Not only would they be worshiping a false god, but by its very name, the false god in question would be pretending to be the Lord God or *Yahweh*.

Israelites erecting these representations of these gods and goddesses in various places in their land are guilty of the highest form of blasphemy and apostasy, and the Israelite prophets do not deal kindly with them, often condemning the rulers who allow such worship to go unchecked.[9] For the devout Israelite, the singular and omnipotent Lord Yahweh not only stands above, beyond, and over the pagan baals and astartes but is the only God, and there are occasions when he sets out to prove it, and for this exercise, especially in the Historical Books of the Bible, he uses his angels.

The relationship between the Chosen People and the Lord's angels is personal, dynamic, and positive. Angels are *not* gods; they are the Lord's messengers who appear in dreams or in human form at select places and times. The book of Judges has plenty examples of these divine messengers. When an angel visits Gideon, he is moved to action in saving the Israelites from the Midianites by first destroying an altar to Baal that his father had built (Judg 6:25-31). When the townspeople want to stone Gideon for this deed, his father defends his son and tells the townspeople that, if Baal is really a god, Baal himself should be able to take revenge. Of course, Baal, being a false god, cannot harm Gideon.

The juxtaposition between the angel's support of Gideon and the Israelites on the one side and the impotence of Baal against the Lord's people on the other exemplifies a theme running through the whole book of Judges. Although the Israelites may apostatize and often do, and although this apostasy fractures their relationship with the Lord God, the baals and the astartes to whom the Israelites turn are ultimately powerless before the Lord and can in no way compete with him.

The Samson cycle (Judg 13–16) begins with the visit of an angel to Samson's father and mother. The mother refers to him as a "man of God," which is another name for a prophet, but she also tells her husband that this man's "appearance was like that of an angel of God" (Judg 13:6). When the angel returns to complete his message about Samson, Manoah tries to persuade him to stay for a meal, but the angel declines, telling Manoah instead to turn the meal into an offering to God. Manoah asks the angel his name; the angel refuses to state it, replying that his name is incomprehensible; and with that, the angel ascends to heaven in the flame of the sacrifice (13:18-20). The lesson to Manoah, the Israelites, and contemporary readers is the same: the Lord is directing this operation, and the angel's identity is solely to be the Lord God's messenger; there are no separate honors for him, and he is not to be confused with the Lord.

If the Israelites fall into apostasy, angels, functioning as messengers, often bring them back to the Lord. The particulars may vary with each passage, but there are three constants in the different accounts. First, the Israelites express a need to the Lord. Second, the Lord responds to the need by sending an angel as a messenger. Third, there is no confusing the angel with any deity; there is only one God, who is the Lord.

1 and 2 Samuel

The books of Samuel relate the rise of the Israelite monarchy first with Saul and then with David. There are no accounts of angel appearances, but there are references to worship of the baals and the astartes.[10] Even the passage describing Saul's "evil spirit" (1 Sam 16:14-23) does not discuss possession by a demon. Rather, the symptoms described most closely resemble clinical depression and bipolarity. Yet, these books contain a very famous and dramatic passage of Saul's consultation with the Medium of Endor (1 Sam 28:8-25).[11] This piece not only serves as the climax to the story of Saul and David but also reveals the application of the laws against the occult.

There are explicit laws against consulting with the dead and necromancy. In Leviticus we read, "Do not turn to mediums or wizards; do not seek them out, to be defiled by them: I am the Lord your God" (19:31), and "A man or a woman who is a medium or a wizard shall be put to death; they shall be stoned to death, their blood is upon them" (20:27). Saul apparently enforces these prescriptions (1 Sam 28:9), yet he violates his own decrees in visiting the medium.

Ironically, the medium is able to conjure up the long-deceased Samuel from Sheol, just as Saul requests, who reiterates what he foretold as a prophet (1 Sam 15); matters for Saul are simply following the course that the Lord has ordained. Yet, the fact that she is able to rouse Samuel would seem to validate the claims of necromancers: they can summon the dead despite the Lord's claim on the universe. Nonetheless, the medium's reaction to seeing Samuel (28:12) confirms the Lord Yahweh as the God of the living and the dead. Samuel is a prophet of the Lord, and the fact that he appears demonstrates that he is acting with the Lord's permission. When the medium shrieks, she acknowledges that she and Saul have gone where they should not have transgressed, and she fears for her own life.[12]

1 Kings

The First Book of Kings is divided between the dynastic history of Judah and Israel (1–16; 20–22) and the stories of the prophets Elijah and Elisha (17–19). There are no angelic appearances.[13] Instead, the text concentrates on the apostasy of the people in running after the false gods and Solomon's guilt in encouraging such apostasy by his marrying so many foreign women.

Solomon has a large harem of foreign wives hailing from Egypt, Moab, Ammon, Edom, Sidon, and Asia Minor (1 Kgs 11:1). These women end up doing what the Lord warned they would do: they turn Solomon toward the strange and false gods (1 Kgs 11:2-10). Three of the gods—Chemosh, Milcom, and Molech—are actually the three different pronunciations of the name of one god in the different lands bordering ancient Israel. Worshiping them is bad enough, but having temples to them within the confines of the Holy City of Jerusalem exacerbates the apostasy, especially since the palace stands next door to Solomon's famous temple to the Lord. Solomon tries to mitigate the offense by building a temple to Chemosh and Molech on a hill opposite Jerusalem for his wives to use (1 Kgs 11:7-8), but it does not erase his apostasy. To this day, that hill is called the "Mount of Scandal." This polytheism entails far greater evils, however. Chemosh, Molech, and Milcom were particularly vicious gods that demanded child sacrifice. If Solomon built "high places" for them, there must have been such reprehensible ritualistic slaughter taking place.

On this point, we come to the greatest visible difference between the worship the Lord required from the Israelites and the worship the gods of the neighboring peoples demanded from their followers. Human sacrifice by law and tradition is absolutely forbidden within the religious tradition outlined in the Old Testament. One of the lessons the Hebrew nation learns from Abraham's near sacrifice of Isaac is that, unlike the gods of the Chosen People's neighbors, the Lord does not demand or want child sacrifice; the story is an action statement (Gen 22:1-18).[14] This point is later codified in the Mosaic Law where it becomes an abhorrent offense to "make[s] a son or daughter pass through fire" (Deut 18:10-13). The prophets Isaiah and Jeremiah particularly rail incessantly against this terrible crime, and the fact that they do indicates that the Israelites must have been practicing it, not only the general population, but the royal house as well.[15]

An explanation as to why the surrounding polytheistic cultures felt so inclined to sacrifice their young is helpful for establishing the context and mindset.

The people dealt with their gods on a *quid pro quo* basis. For example, a particular god would guarantee a bountiful harvest if it in turn received tribute. The tribute could be the firstfruits of the harvest, a choice animal, or any other precious and prized possession. The logic continues right up the chain, for what could be more precious than one's children or loved ones? The people were only doing what they thought they had to do, as gruesome as it was. Their religion was not based on divine revelation, as the Israelites claim that their faith was. This situation, however, also serves as a foil to the requirements of the Israelite faith.

Starting with the covenant made with Abraham (Gen 15:1-21; 17:1-15) and continuing with Moses at the burning bush (Exod 3:4-15) and atop Mount Sinai (Exod 19–20), the Lord God establishes a loving relationship with his people, and the people are to respond in kind by remaining faithful to that covenant. This mutual relationship is not *quid pro quo*. Even when the people forsake the covenant—and they constantly do—the Lord remains faithful and calls them back. In terms of how this relationship is expressed cultically, sacrifice of the children is forbidden, and a firstborn animal is substituted. Moreover, even that custom will eventually evolve from animal offerings to grain offerings to following moral prescripts.

For the present purpose of defining the line separating Judaism and Christianity[16] from polytheistic claims on the universe, and thus developing a theology that encompasses both demons and angels, it is essential to understand the crucial role that revelation plays. Ancient Israel's neighbors worship the creature and not the creator, whereas the Israelites, as inheritors of the revealed covenant, worship the creator and not the creature. There will be more about this point below.

Elijah and the prophets of Baal. Elijah's contest with the prophets of Baal (1 Kgs 18) provides us with a snapshot of the differences between the Lord God and the storm god, Baal. The king of the Northern Kingdom of Israel, Ahab, is married to Jezebel, the daughter of the Sidonian king, Ethbaal (1 Kgs 16:31).[17] Jezebel brings in all the idols, false gods, and prophets along with her entourage. Unlike Solomon and his foreign wives, however, Jezebel does not merely worship the baals on her own; she enforces her religion on the whole land and persecutes the prophets of the Lord God and all other followers as well, and Ahab follows along with her.

Because of this situation, the land becomes cursed with a drought that only Elijah the prophet can lift. In order to show King Ahab and the general population the fallacy of the baals, Elijah organizes a contest on Mount Carmel where he alone challenges the "four hundred and fifty prophets of Baal and the four hundred prophets of Asherah who eat at Jezebel's table" (1 Kgs 18:19). Each group is to sacrifice a bull, Baal's prophets to Baal, and Elijah to the Lord God. The scene that follows provides a glimpse into pagan religious practices of that age vis-à-vis those of the Israelite prophet Elijah.

The contest is for everyone to witness who is the true God, the Lord or Baal. The prophets of Baal keep repeating the call, "O Baal, answer us!" to no avail (1 Kgs 18:26). Scholars interpret their "hopping" around the altar as some kind of ritualized dance used to get the deity's attention. This dance is combined with the blood from their self-lashing and gashing. The pain combined with the frenzied dance leads to an excited, prophetic state (1 Kgs 18:28-29). They have been performing this ritual since early morning and enduring Elijah's taunts the whole time but to no avail.

There are subtle yet important differences in the way Elijah handles the problem of igniting his sacrificial fire. The twelve stones for the altar recall the Israelites' covenant with the Lord. The slaughtered bull, the wood, and the altar are drenched with water three times (1 Kgs 18:30-35). Elijah's prayer is direct and succinct. The Lord's relationship with his people is emphasized by naming "Abraham, Isaac, and Israel [=Jacob]." Finally, Elijah states in everyone's hearing, "let it be known this day that you are God in Israel, that I am your servant, and that I have done all these things at your bidding" (1 Kgs 18:36). This last sentence is important. Elijah is not trying to control or manipulate the Lord as the pagan prophets try to do to Baal, "O Baal, answer us!" (1 Kgs 18:26). Rather, the Lord God is in charge of everything, and Elijah is his instrument (1 Kgs 18:1-2), and this is the point that Elijah wants all to see.

The competition between Baal and the Lord for the people's hearts continues into 2 Kings. Elijah intercepts messengers that Ahaziah sends to Ekron for consultation with Baal-zebub. Because Ahaziah apostatizes in this manner, he brings about his own death (2 Kgs 1:16). Meanwhile, the pagan Naaman, because he seeks out Elisha for a cure, is healed of his leprosy. Naaman even acknowledges that the Lord God stands above the whole earth and has no equal (2 Kgs 5:1-15). The story uses the foreigner, Naaman, who has benefited from the one and true Lord God, to assert the monotheistic faith of Israel in light of the polytheistic beliefs surrounding God's people.

Tobit

Although part of the canon for the Roman Catholic and Greek Orthodox traditions, Tobit is included as apocryphal material in most Protestant Bibles. It reads like a religious novel, and, for our purposes, it is most interesting because the archangel Raphael plays a major role, as does the demon Asmodeus.

This discussion will concentrate on only these two characters and, interestingly, the dog.

Separated by distance but unknowingly related by blood, both Tobit and Sarah are suffering, he from blindness and she from sevenfold widowhood; each of Sarah's husbands dies before the marriage is consummated. Tobit and Sarah pray to God for death. God heeds their prayers and sends the angel Raphael to remedy both situations. Raphael will cure Tobit's blindness and drive out from Sarah's house the wicked demon Asmodeus who is responsible for killing Sarah's husbands on their wedding night (Tob 3:16-17). Tobit sends his son Tobias to Media to collect a sum of money and pays Raphael, disguised as his kinsman Azariah, to accompany him. Tobit's wife Anna is inconsolable, fearing she will never see her son alive again. When Tobias and Raphael walk out the door, the dog follows (6:1).

With Raphael's help, Tobias arrives in Media carrying with him the heart, liver, and gall of a large fish that had tried to swallow his foot while Tobias was bathing in the Tigris River. Upon entering the house of Raguel, Sarah's father, they are treated to the customary hospitality feast. Raguel overhears that Tobias is interested in marrying Sarah, and Raguel seals the marriage contract that night (7:9-16). Heeding Raphael's instructions (Tob 6), Tobias and Sarah burn the heart and liver on the incense pot as soon as they enter the bridal chamber. The stench drives away the demon Asmodeus, who flees to upper Egypt. Raphael pursues him there and binds him hand and foot. Raphael returns immediately. Meanwhile, before engaging in sexual intercourse, the couple pray (8:1-8). Raphael, Tobias, and now Sarah return to Nineveh, and as they leave, the dog once again follows (11:4).

When Raphael, Tobias, and Sarah arrive at the home of Tobit and Anna, Tobias applies the remaining fish gall to Tobit's eyes, and he regains his sight. Raphael then reveals his true identity: "it was I who presented and read the record of your prayer before the glory of the Lord; and likewise whenever you would bury the dead. . . . I am Raphael, one of the seven angels who stand ready and enter before the glory of the Lord" (12:12, 15).[1]

Tobit is a late book within the canon; scholars date its writing to about 200 BC. In dealing with the subject of angels and demons, therefore, it is very helpful in giving us a glimpse of how the Jews of that time interpreted the presence of demons and angels. The demon is called Asmodeus; this name surfaces again in our studies. Asmodeus is also exorcised from the chamber with smoke, though foul-smelling, and Raphael pursues him and *binds* him.

On the other hand, angels, as seen with Raphael, are categorized according to their duties; Raphael, for instance, is one of the seven angels who "stand[s] ready and enter[s] before the glory of the Lord" (12:15). Moreover, angels have a direct contact with God and do everything he wishes and commands (12:14).

Before Tobit dies, he gives advice to his son Tobias. He tells him to take his family and flee Nineveh for Media where he will be safe in the face of Nineveh's impending doom (14:4). Tobit also relates that his countrymen and countrywomen in Israel will be scattered and exiled from their homeland. Drawing on prophetic literature, Tobit also acknowledges the restoration of Israel and her vocation to the rest of humankind: "Then the nations in the whole world will all be converted and worship God in truth. They will all abandon their idols, which deceitfully have led them into their error" (14:6).

Tobit's deathbed prediction introduces a new element into the traditional Israelite interpretation of the idol worship as practiced by Israel's neighbors. Not only does idol worship represent obeisance to a counterfeit deity, but the idols themselves have deceived people with lies, falsehood, and error. Tobit holds that the pagan nations of the world deserve better, and one day they too will turn to God in true worship. The connection of polytheistic idols with deceit, however, is a step toward tying them to the realm of the diabolical and demonic.

The two references of the unnamed and ever-faithful pet dog in Tobit are the only two positive accounts of a dog in all of Scripture; every other verse mentioning a dog is a curse or a pejorative statement. The writer of Tobit implies the presence of God's protection through one of God's creatures. It is not an exaggeration to say that the dog, in assisting Raphael in his care, is a sacramental element confirming how all the earth reflects the glory of the Lord, and the treatment of that canine in this text has implications for how humans treat God's other creatures.

Chapter 2

Wisdom Books

The Wisdom Books

The wisdom genre is common to many cultures of the ancient world and is known by its practical application of devotion to the divine. With aphorisms, examples, and theological speculation, Wisdom treats the nature of good and evil, theodicy, immortality, and the meaning of life. Attributed to Solomon, the various books within this section date from various periods within Israel's history. The monotheistic character of the writings manifests itself by emphasizing the teaching of the law and the prophets as true wisdom, and abandonment of that tradition as absolute folly. The highest wisdom then becomes associated with the Wisdom of God, which in turn is the creative and guiding Word in the universe. Folly and ignorance, therefore, are the polar opposite of a life faithful to the Lord God leading to an impiety directed toward death.

The Book of Job

The book of Job opens the collection known as the Wisdom Books. For our purposes, the name "Satan" as a proper noun in the Old Testament corpus first arises in the book of Job.[2] In these opening verses, Satan is in the heavenly court and takes his instructions and leave from God (1:6-12). Although Satan causes a great deal of misery and pain for Job, his doubts about Job and his acts against him are directed toward showing the greater glory of God. God is the one who calls attention to Job's righteousness, and Satan is the one who tests the depth of Job's devotion for the whole heavenly court. In the end, Job by his faithfulness and endurance proves God right and Satan wrong.

The Book of Psalms

This hymnbook of ancient Israel is replete with verses and allusions to foreign nations and their respective gods, gods who fall far short in the power, ability, care, and concern of the God of Israel. Taking these references as a collective understanding of the polytheistic world surrounding Israel does not lead to any single conclusion. On the one hand, the psalmist will assert the Lord God as the sole ruler of the universe and a loving one at that. Indeed, this theme dominates the whole book. On the other hand, there are many references that acknowledge that the foreign nations have their own gods and that these gods sit in the "divine council" with the God of Israel. These texts witness to the existence of *monolatry* in the ancient world and, in Israel's case, the movement from monolatry to monotheism. In monolatry, every nation has its own gods, which people of other nations do not recognize. In the examples cited here, Israel champions the Lord God before whom all other gods lapse into insignificance. While this vacillation between monolatry and monotheism in the faith life of ancient Israel may be confusing, it actually reflects the peoples' growth in their understanding of their faith.[3]

The foreign gods, though not equal to the Lord God, nonetheless exercise their authority, albeit badly, and if called to demonstrate their power, they are generally impotent and unresponsive (see Pss 16, 58, 82, 84, 86, 96, 97, 106, 135, 136).

Psalm 106 in particular connects these lesser gods to evil. The Israelite apostasy in the desert is described in terms linking the practices of the sinners within the midst of God's people as engaged in worshiping the dead (106:28) and, even more seriously, sacrificing their sons and daughters to these foreign deities (106:37). The description of these heinous practices are in line with the narratives in the books of Samuel and Kings, and because the Psalms are the prayers of the Israelites, if they are not descriptive of the way things were, they are normative of the way things ought to be.

The Book of Proverbs

The well-known verse, "The fear of the Lord is the beginning of knowledge" (Prov 1:7), introduces the reader to the path of right living. The way to success in this life is tied to a strong devotion to the Lord. The nearly constant repetition of the "fear of the Lord" melds this disposition of heart and mind with practical deeds of daily life. Moreover, good quotidian habits are never divorced from justice, diligence for the good, and compassion toward one's neighbor. Specifically, prayer and devotion to the Lord must include all the suffering in God's creation; on Sinai, God revealed himself to the whole community as one people, not to isolated individuals. Preferring folly and ignorance leads to abomination, a sin which is an attitude that not only rejects the law but also leads to such a flagrant violation of the law that "The devising of folly is sin, and the scoffer is an abomination to all" (Prov 24:9). These are the ones "who forsake the paths of uprightness to walk in the ways of darkness, who rejoice in doing evil and delight in the perverseness of evil" (Prov 2:13-14).

Throughout Proverbs, children are admonished time and time again to avoid walking the path of the wicked, and to describe the wicked, their actions, and the inevitable outcome of their deeds, the writer employs language that resonates with what we have already seen in the Old Testament. Among the descriptors are "evildoers," "violence," "darkness," "crooked speech," and "devious talk." Contrasted with these ways of Lady Folly and in language that encourages and cajoles the reader are the means and ends of Lady Wisdom: "path of the righteous," "Light of dawn," and "straight path" (Prov 4:18, 26).

Wisdom of Solomon

The Wisdom of Solomon, more than any other of the Wisdom books, situates the paths and actions of the wicked within their proper realm; they are under the thrall of death: "Do not invite death by the error of your life, or bring on destruction by the works of your hands; because God did not make death, and does not delight in the death of the living. For he created all things so that they might exist; the generative forces of the world are wholesome, and there is not destructive poison in them, and the dominion of Hades is not on earth. Righteousness itself is immortal" (Wis 1:12-15). Death is personified (Wis 1:16), and all life, all human experience, is but a futile, hopeless enterprise (Wis 2:1-11).

The remarkable feature of the Wisdom of Solomon, originally written in Greek without an earlier Hebrew text, lies in its role of providing so much of the blueprint for the passion narratives in the gospels, particularly the Synoptics. Whole sections, such as Wisdom 2:12-20, resemble the Suffering Servant passages in Isaiah. The conceit in Wisdom shows evildoers lying in wait for the righteous man in order to torture and put him to death (2:20). These purveyors of evil find him inconvenient because he opposes their actions and reproaches them (Wis 2:12). The evil ones are never named; nonetheless, they represent everything militating against the good, and in this sense, the biblical narrative differentiates the lines between good and evil. That ultimate evil, namely, death, enters the world because of the devil's envy (Wis 2:24). The righteous, however, despite all appearances to the contrary, will not succumb to this evil death (Wis 3:1-9).

The Wisdom of Solomon also introduces the Last Judgment into the biblical narrative. It is a scene in which the deeds and machinations of the evildoers against the righteous disappear and have no effect. Their great punishment comes when they face the righteous and see for themselves the futility of their actions. Indeed, it is they, the evildoers, who are "consumed in [their] wickedness" (Wis 5:13). The righteous, on the other hand, live forever, defended by the Lord who uses righteousness, justice, and holiness as his primary weapons against evil (Wis 5:15-20).

The Wisdom of Solomon, in discussing the punishment of the wicked, includes animal worship among their sins (11:15). Moreover, the writer combines these sins with other Old Testament abominations ascribed to the Israelites' contemporaries and erstwhile neighbors. These sins consist of those mentioned in Exodus and Deuteronomy: sorcery and child and human sacrifice (Wis 12:3-6). To make the point, the Wisdom text compares and contrasts the worship of nature with the true worship of God. Practitioners of the former have mistaken the creature for the creator, and the writer appeals to them to look to God the creator as the one responsible for the beautiful creation and to direct their worship accordingly (Wis 13–15). Idolatry is a great lie that spawns all other evils such as infanticide, adultery, fornication, and murder (Wis 14:23-26). God, however, is "kind and true," and to know him and his power is the righteousness that leads to immortality (Wis 15:1-3).

The writer of Wisdom delineates a sharp division between idolatry and the true worship of God. Idolatry limits worship to creatures, whether those creatures be trees, animals, other humans, or handmade forms. Because the object of worship is the creature, the object and the worshiper suffer death and decay, the fate of every created thing. Since worship is supposed to extend to existence beyond the self and idolatry does not do that, it is false, and this falsehood has dire consequences in that it ultimately leads to more lies as well as suffering and death.

The true worship of God, on the other hand, has as its object a living and loving person beyond created matter. In fact, the object is the Creator himself. Because such worship is directed beyond this created realm, it is true. This true worship conducts the worshiper along the true path of righteousness, goodness, and life; true worship ultimately leads to life, not death. In sum, God is life, and false gods are death.

The Book of Sirach

Sirach, the most extensive of the Wisdom books, while saying little about Satan, the devil, and demons, discusses sin, anger, and injustice as the enemy of Wisdom and thus of God (1:22-30). The identification of Wisdom with God is the major focus of the Wisdom Books in general; Sirach is true to the genre. The phrase "fear of the LORD" or "fear of God" describes the proper intellectual and emotional posture a person must possess when facing God, and it is often misunderstood.

God is totally other. Human beings cannot make, shape, or distort God. "Fear of God" is the stance before the Divine that demonstrates an awe toward the majesty that belongs to God alone. It is a healthy fear that does not flee because of the terror or destruction the other might use to strike, for God does not annihilate. Rather, God calls one to change, repent, and renew. These are actions that can remake an individual, and they can be daunting and frightening, but they are always good. "Fear of God" is true worship and true humility. On the other hand, the false worship of idols leads to humiliation.

Sirach launches into an excursus comparing false worship with true (Sir 34). With strong warning against trusting in dreams, the writer connects dreams with idolatry. Such a negative picture of dreams may seem odd to many in light of the fact that so many of the personages of the Bible receive divine communication from dreams. Abraham, Jacob, Joseph, Peter, and Paul all hear their respective commands from God through a dream or trance, while Sirach states, "Divination, omens and dreams all are unreal . . . the mind has fantasies (Sir 34:5). Further on, however, Sirach advises, "Unless they are sent by intervention from the Most High, pay no attention to them. For dreams have deceived many, and those who put their hope in them have perished" (Sir 34:6-7). For Sirach, then, the object and source of prayer must always be God. Anything less than that is false and empty.

Within Christianity, dreams, visions, apparitions, and such have had a long history; in fact, they are very biblical in nature. Determining whether or not a vision comes from God requires a strong prayer life and connection to the faith community and its Tradition. Just as all the great mystics and saints sought the assistance and confidence of an experienced, spiritual guide, those today who believe the Holy Spirit is communicating with them in a similar way should "Test the spirits" (1 John 4:1) with a trusted and experienced spiritual director.

Chapter 3

Isaiah the Prophet

The prophetic literature is one of the main genres of the Christian Old Testament. While it contains many historical references, and while scholars can situate each book within a particular historical time and place, the message of prophesy moves beyond an enumeration of historical occurrences. Likewise, biblical prophecy does not foretell some future event known to no one but the prophet speaking. Prophecy is not fortunetelling. Rather, prophecy interprets a series of past and contemporary events and explains their influence on the current or future situation. How prophecy relates to the interplay of diabolical and angelic forces, therefore, depends in large part on how humans maintain their relationship to God. The prophets do not mention demons, the devil, or unclean spirits. Rather, the prophetic literature as a whole chastizes the people for idol worship and all the sins such worship entails. Some examples from Isaiah make this point clearer.

Isaiah

The book of the Prophet Isaiah provides some of the best examples of interpreting the good and evil actions undertaken by people ostensibly devoted to serving God. There are seven sections from this book that elucidate the distinction between worship of the God of Israel from the gods of Israel's neighbors. Moreover, worship of the foreign gods always implies cavorting with demons.

Isaiah 7

This short chapter provides an excellent example of prophetic word and action along with a very rare display of a prophet's discretion. King Ahaz is notorious for engaging in child sacrifice (see 2 Kgs 16:1-5). Here, without it being specifically mentioned, he has just performed the abominable deed. The Israelite kingdom in the north has allied itself with Syria to attack King Ahaz of Judah. Ahaz and the people are petrified. Rather than trusting in the Lord, however, Ahaz resorts to sacrificing his son in the fuller's field with hopes of currying the Lord's favor in the same manner that Judah's neighbors aim to please their bloodthirsty gods.

In a masterful stroke of tact, Isaiah accuses Ahaz of such an abomination by standing along the road while the king passes by. Isaiah's own young son Shearjashub is at the prophet's side, and the road itself is one coming from the fuller's field, i.e., the scene of the crime. Ahaz knows that Isaiah knows, and therefore the Lord knows that the king has sacrificed his son. When Isaiah tells Ahaz to ask for a sign from the Lord, he is actually telling him to put his whole trust in the Lord. Ahaz refuses the forgiveness that the Lord, through Isaiah, offers because he considers himself unworthy of forgiveness. This hard-hearted stance causes Isaiah to seek the sign for Ahaz: the king's young wife will bear another son who will succeed the father (7:13-14).

Isaiah 45–46 presents an interface between the Lord and the gods of Israel's enemies. Within the discourse, Isaiah claims the sovereignty of God over all creation by emphasizing the fact that the Lord God *made* and *fashioned* all creatures as well as the earth; as a pot cannot rule the potter, neither can creatures

control their creators (45:9-12). Isaiah continues by declaring
to all the unbelieving nations that their gods are useless as he
invites them to set down those idols and turn to the true God,
Lord, and creator (45:20-25).

As the book of the Prophet Isaiah reaches its conclusion, the
distinction between idol worship, falsehood, sin, and death on
the one side with social justice and life on the other is brought
into high relief (57–59). Devotion to idols has brought the
people to the abominable practice of child sacrifice (57:1-10),
even as these false gods deliver nothing but empty promises and
vain hopes (57:11-13). For those who follow the Lord, the
discourse clarifies the difference between true and false worship.
Any practice that does not free captives from oppression, feed
the hungry, house the homeless, clothe the naked is false worship even if directed toward the true God (58:3-7). Attention
to and help for the suffering will lead the people to the fulfillment of the Lord God's covenant (58:13-14). Furthermore,
turning away from idols and toward the true Lord God, coupled
with concerns for social justice, will see the ingathering and
redemption of all peoples along with Israel (60–61). God the
Creator and Lord will then lead all to a glorious and new creation where justice will reign, suffering will cease, and evil will
vanish (65:17-25).

Summary

In Genesis we see two trajectories. In one, evil and sin are
independent of the Lord God, who is always seen as a loving
God. The Lord God establishes a covenant with Abraham that
extends to all his descendants through Isaac, the son of his
wife, Sarah. These descendants frequently are faithless and run
after false gods. In the second trajectory, evil and sin are
equated with these false gods who demand sinful behavior on
the part of the Israelites, especially that great abomination,
child sacrifice.

As the tradition develops, the prohibition against worshiping false gods melds with false worship of the true Lord God; specifically, worship of the Lord God must entail concerns of social justice. Any form of worship that ignores the plight of the widow, orphan, stranger, homeless, or naked blasphemes the loving God. Worship of false gods along with false worship of the true Lord God is sin, and sin is death, suffering, and evil. Quite simply, worship of the Lord God leads to life, whereas worship of false gods leads to death. Moreover, as we see in the prophet Isaiah, the day will come when the life and goodness the Lord God offers his Chosen People will extend to all nations.

Chapter 4

New Testament

The devil, Satan, demons, and unclean spirits receive more attention and press in the New Testament than they do in the Old Testament. By the time Jesus arrives on the scene, the connection between false gods and their evil influence is well established, at least among the pious. We return to what we said at the beginning of this study, and that is the overriding understanding within Christianity that Christ, by his incarnation, passion, death, and resurrection, rescues all creation from the thrall of Satan and death. Moreover, this victory of Christ's is irreversible, and we live within this redeemed ambit until today.

The Gospels

Each of the gospels shows Christ encountering demons, Satan, and evil spirits in some way, be it exorcising someone possessed or curing a person of disease or infirmity. Some of these stories are common to all four accounts (Matthew, Mark, Luke, John), and others are restricted to a certain gospel alone. In the following section, I concentrate on those passages that illustrate two points. The first shows Jesus in a battle with evil, supernatural forces for control of the world and universe, and the second presents Jesus as curing the sick whose suffering is indicative of a world incomplete in its final union with God and God's goodness.

Cosmic Battle with Satan

In all four gospels there is very little difference, if any, between the terms "the devil," "evil one," and "Satan." The being is the one and the same master of evil and all things diabolical.[1] Satan's rule is diametrically opposed to God's, and with Christ's birth and ministry, Satan meets his greatest threat. The reader also encounters such terms as "demon" and "unclean spirit." Here too, the words are synonymous. They are evil, supernatural beings subservient to their master, Satan. In the New Testament, their presence in the world causes harm and suffering from which only the goodness of Christ can deliver one. In their arrogance, they will also try to trip up, always unsuccessfully, the Savior of the world, Jesus Christ.

Temptation of Jesus in the Desert
(Matt 4:1-11; Mark 1:12-13; Luke 4:1-13)

In all three accounts, the temptation in the desert occurs immediately or nearly so after Jesus' baptism. Since the baptism in each case initiates his earthly ministry, Satan (or the Devil, Evil One) attempts to thwart the divine plan. Mark paints the most stark and dramatic picture of all the versions; it is also the shortest. The operative point in the description is that the "Spirit immediately drove [Jesus] out into the wilderness" (1:12). That it is the Holy Spirit and not a malevolent being who pushes Jesus into the wasteland is very important. God is in control and is not subject to anyone or anything. If Jesus heads into the desert, it is part of the divine plan, not because some contrary power assumes control even for a minute.

But why the temptation? The particulars vary from gospel to gospel, but we can make the categorical statement that, in each case, the Evangelist is setting the stage for the cosmic battle for the final redemption of God's creation. Throughout the gospels, opposition to Jesus' mission is cast as the work of the Evil One who relies on sickness, disease, demonic possession, and political conspiracy against Jesus to halt the spread of the kingdom of God. Having the temptation at the beginning of the earthly ministry shows how seriously the powers of darkness take the threat of Jesus' promise of the new reign of God.

As a location, the desert is a place where life and death hang in a balance. Often called the "wilderness" in the gospels to distinguish the geography from the Arabian Desert further south of Judea, the "wilderness" most likely refers to what is now known as the Negev Desert. It is an area east of Jerusalem and Bethlehem and extends as far as the southern end of the Dead Sea, where it is called the *Arava*. Nonetheless, exactly where Jesus went is impossible to determine, and it is also possible that he went to the Sinai, which would certainly have historical and theological significance. In any case, such a land possesses little if any water, extreme temperatures, and bands of roaming jackals and hyenas as well as brigands and murderers.

Jackals and hyenas, because they prey on the weak, sick, and dying and, most important, because they eat carrion, have long been associated with death, and death in both the Jewish and Christian traditions is the result of sin and separation from God and all goodness. Their threatening presence, combined with their ominous and feral cries, has contributed to their long association with the demonic realm. In this context, for Jesus to be with the "wild beasts" is for him to be surrounded by the forces of Satan. The gospels of Matthew and Mark mention that angels come and minister to Jesus. This is a detail absent in Luke at the temptation.[2]

A more elaborate temptation scene is found in both Matthew and Luke. These two accounts feature a threefold temptation of Jesus: to turn stones into bread, to show off his divinity in front of spectators, and to gain earthly power and glory (though in Luke the temptations are in a slightly different order from Matthew). These temptations are a form of idol worship. By turning stones into bread, Jesus would be using his divine nature for his own personal advantage; by casting himself off the pinnacle of the temple, he would use his divinity for his own greater glory; and by worshiping Satan to gain earthly power, he would be worshiping a false god.

This last form of temptation especially ties into our earlier discussion on idol worship as a turning from the creator in favor of the creature. With each of the evangelists, for Jesus to succumb would make him guilty of scamming hypocrisy, and his whole earthly mission would be confounded.

Jesus and Beelzebul
(Matt 12:22-32; Mark 3:22-30; Luke 11:14-23)

The scene in each of the three Synoptic Gospels is similar. Jesus performs miracles, exorcises demons, and cures illnesses. The people have never witnessed such occurrences before, and they realize that they are in the presence of a definite supernatural force. The controversy arises when leaders from Jerusalem arrive and ascribe the powerful deeds not to God but to Beelzebul.[3]

This passage serves to clarify everything about the cosmic battle we have said thus far. In his explanation, Jesus turns to the parable about the strong man. Here, the *strong man* represents Beelzebul or Satan, and his house stands for the world. The understanding is that up to the moment of Jesus' arrival, Satan has the world in his clutches. Now that Jesus is on the scene, that situation changes. Of all the evangelists, Luke describes Jesus' actions the best.

In Luke, Jesus is the "one stronger" who attacks the "strong man" (Satan), overpowers him (despite the armor in which the strong man trusted), and divides the strong man's plunder. The use of the term "plunder" shows that everything in the strong man's house is ill-gotten and never his in the first place. Included as "plunder" are the people as well as everything else in God's creation. In Mark and Matthew, Jesus "binds" Satan, whereas in Luke, Jesus "overpowers" him. The use of "overpower" is more correct in describing Jesus' mission in that the verb carries a more intensive and definitive meaning; Satan or Beelzebul has lost all ability to dominate, and the world rightly belongs to God and his kingdom.[4]

The Gerasene (Gadarene) Demoniac
(Matt 8:28-34; Mark 5:1-20; Luke 8:26-39)

There is probably no other story in the New Testament that has fascinated and frightened more people than the exorcism of the Gerasene demoniac. That there are variations of the account points to the hold it has had on Christians since the writing of the gospels. For example, Matthew reads "two demoniacs" (8:28), and a number of ancient manuscripts define the locale as either *Gerasene* or *Gadarene* territory.[5] As often happens in the retelling of an important story, minor details may shift, but the important points remain solidly in place, and such occurs here.

The possessed man exhibits phenomenal strength. Neither shackles nor chains nor other individuals can restrain him; people avoid walking anywhere near him. The demoniac lives in tombs with the dead. He is naked, and he shrieks and howls. Yet, when he sees Jesus, he recognizes him as the "Son of the Most High God" (Luke 8:28). Jesus recognizes the demoniac for what he is as well: a man possessed by an unclean spirit (Luke 8:29).

Mark and Luke have Jesus questioning the possessed man, and from this short dialogue, we learn that the demon's name is "Legion," along with the explanation that there are many demons possessing the man, an allusion to the number of soldiers comprising a Roman legion, about fifty-two hundred men. Since the Romans were Gentiles who worshiped false gods, to a Jewish audience, the name "Legion" would confirm everything they thought and feared, i.e., the Romans were in league with the devil. Similarly, early Gentile Christians would draw the same conclusion, for the Romans persecuted the Christians until Constantine issued the Edict of Milan in 313.

A remarkable feature in all three versions of this story is that the man or the demons ask Jesus to be sent into the nearby swine. Matthew does not give a reason for this request, but one unclean spirit in Mark begs Jesus not to send the demons "out of the country" (5:10), while in Luke all the demons beseech Jesus not to send them "back into the abyss" (8:31). Whether the request is to stay in the country or not to go back into the abyss, the accounts show that the demons know that Jesus is ultimately their master. These unclean spirits do not call upon Beelzebul or Satan to come to their aid; to do so would be a useless venture, and they know it.

Even more interesting is why these demons do not want to return whence they came. The "abyss," a bottomless pit in Greek, is the place of hopelessness, despair, terror, and pain. The "abyss" is very much like many of our traditional ideas of hell, and the demons do not want to be there either. A conclusion from this interchange is that dwelling with the devil is a terrible existence even for those spirits allied with him; demons suffer from being around other demons; they are not any more pleasant to each other than they are to the ones they possess.

Jesus grants them their request to enter the swine. To a Jewish audience, swine are notoriously unclean animals, and to be associated with them would itself be a curse. The unclean spirits flee to unclean animals who rush down the mountainside into the Sea of Galilee where they drown. Ironically, large bodies of water at this time, for both Gentiles and Jews, represent the bottomless, boundless abyss, or the abode of all hopelessness.

The story of the Gerasene demoniac connects with the account of Jesus and Beelzebul. The latter account ends with Jesus telling the people that every sin will be forgiven except blasphemy against the Holy Spirit. The demons demonstrate such blasphemy. Throughout their encounter with Jesus, they show that they know he is the Son of the Most High God. They ask him not to send them to the hateful abyss, and they beg him to let them go into the swine. They know that he is the Lord. What they do not do is ask to become clean, to be forgiven, to become one with him. The blasphemy against the Holy Spirit is to recognize the Lordship of Christ but not to accept the love and forgiveness he offers. There cannot be forgiveness if one refuses the forgiveness that Christ extends.

Writings of Saint Paul

Saint Paul gives us one of the clearest perspectives on good and evil supernatural beings in both the Old and New Testaments. While nearly all scholars agree that Paul himself wrote Romans, 1 and 2 Corinthians, Galatians, Philippians, 2 Thessalonians, and Philemon, they disagree over whether Paul or his disciples wrote the rest of the letters attributed to him. This second category, often called the deutero-Pauline works, contain Ephesians, Colossians, 1 Thessalonians, 1 and 2 Timothy, and Titus.

Despite the lack of scholarly consensus on the Pauline corpus, for the purposes of discussing the treatment of angels and demons in the Bible, we can consider all these works as Pauline. Most of the Pauline literature simply references angels and demons as a matter of course, with the exception of two passages, 1 Corinthians 10:14-29 (and its lead in [1 Cor 8:4]) and Colossians 2:16-20, which offer warnings about involvement with idols and spirits. The so-called Letter to the Hebrews is most likely a homily and not a letter, has no affiliation with Paul, and does not address the angelic or demonic worlds.

1 Corinthians 10:14-29

In this passage, Paul addresses a pastoral concern for the Corinthian community, and in so doing, he outlines a theology and practice that is still applicable today regarding moral behavior. The situation is a delicate one. In the pagan areas, the meat of animals offered as sacrifice to the local pagan deities found its way to the market and was sold there. It was simply a matter of economy and the avoidance of waste. The Christian converts still associated with their non-Christian friends and families, however, and at these dinners, this sacrificed meat from the market ended up on the dinner table. The question put to Paul was whether Christians in conscience should still eat the meat, given the fact that it originally came from pagan idol worship.

Paul does not give a simple answer in either the affirmative or the negative; the intent of the Christian involved becomes the determining factor, as well as the understanding of other Christians gathered at the same table. In other words, Paul tells the community member to ask the question, "Why am I doing what I am doing?" If the purpose is simply to be hospitable, it is not a problem, and with that advice Paul attaches a reason: "for 'the earth and its fullness are the Lord's' " (1 Cor 10:26). Here, Paul underscores that the Lord God is the sole master of the universe; demons are inconsequential interlopers. On the other hand, if the purpose of eating the meat is precisely because it has been offered to idols, the answer changes.

Paul's treatment of the question regarding meat offered to idols contains a valuable, pastoral lesson as well as insight on the status of demons in the created universe. Pastorally, he shows regard for the intention behind the act, itself a fundamental point of Christian moral behavior. As for demons, Paul seems to recognize their presence, but he does not credit them with much power or influence outside anyone invoking them through some kind of worship, as in eating the meat offered to idols.

Colossians 2:16-20

> Therefore do not let anyone condemn you in matters of food and drink or of observing festivals, new moons, or sabbaths. These are only a shadow of what is to come, but the substance belongs to Christ. Do not let anyone disqualify you, insisting on self-abasement and worship of angels, dwelling on visions, puffed up without cause by a human way of thinking, and not holding fast to the head, from whom the whole body, nourished and held together by its ligaments and sinews, grows with a growth that is from God. If with Christ you died to the elemental spirits of the universe, why do you live as if you still belonged to the world? Why do you submit to regulations? (Col 2:16-20)

For Paul, the lordship of Christ is everything; there can be no compromise. Salvation has been determined through him, remains in him, and will ever so be. The reading in Colossians attempts to clarify this position, and in its attempt, it draws on both the biblical and Hellenistic worldviews; then, as now, culture and theology were intertwined.

While the letter eschews adherence to the Jewish law at that time, it also addresses the polytheistic claims and practices of the Greco-Roman world. Followers of Christ should not engage in either belief system. The Letter to the Colossians tackles the efficacy of the Jewish law in 2:8-16, and in verses 17-20 moves, almost imperceptibly, into questions of pagan religions with the phrase, "elemental powers of the world." Just what this phrase signifies is difficult to determine absolutely.

The Greek term for "elemental powers" is *stoicheion*, a word that means foundational elements from which everything is made. The context would seem to suggest that the text admonishes against the construction of the universe based on Stoic principles. Yet, text reads the "regulations" (v. 20) as an allusion to the Jewish law, if "festivals, new moons, and Sabbaths" are seen as its referent. Since Colossians stresses the primacy of the Cosmic Christ, it would seem that the writer (Paul?) would link all competing belief systems, considering them bogus inasmuch as they all counter Christ.

Taking into account the Stoic context of the passage, the argument is that anything less than a total life in Christ is entry into the realm of some power or powers that constitute debasement of the human person. Judging from this text, life in Christ is goodness and dignity, and every other claim of salvation is counterfeit at the least and slavery at the most.

The way this passage from Colossians downplays Judaism and non-monotheistic belief systems seems harsh and intolerant to our twenty-first-century ears. Nevertheless, it reflects the mentality of someone besieged by more powerful forces. Such is the story of nascent Christianity; early believers were threatened from above by the Roman Empire's culture and show of force and from below by those who would want converts to become Jews first before becoming Christian. The writer wants to encourage those feeling threatened while discouraging others from relenting in their belief.

If we can sift through the rhetoric, however, Colossians can provide us with the Christian view of the universe that is absolutely unique to Christianity, and it returns to one of the essential points of Christian claims, the incarnation: *Christ, the son of God, has taken on human flesh and thus has sanctified all the created world*. To ascribe to any other supernatural power ownership and allegiance or deference mocks Christ, the true Lord of the universe, by substituting a counterfeit deity, and a malevolent one at that.

Does such a statement mean that every supernatural manifestation outside of Christ is malevolent? Well, yes and no. Yes, when it is outside Christ and is death dealing. Any power that calls forth hatred, suffering, and death is malevolent. There are still places where people engage in the torture and death of both animals and humans either as part of their religion or as secularism masking as religion. These practices are outside of Christ and are evil.

On the other hand, if a supernatural power gives evidence of benevolence and goodness, it is part of the reign of God, and Christians know it when they see it. For example, Christians venerate holy places in nature, e.g., Lourdes, as well as sites where something holy has happened, as with shrines to martyrs, e.g., Thomas à Becket, and places where the holy has become manifest, e.g., the Basilica of the Resurrection in Jerusalem or Saint Francis's town of Assisi. There might not be an explicit reference to Christ in some of these places, but the goodness, the redemption, and the mercy they evoke are implicit connections to Christ. Sometimes these places exist in nature, and Christians will turn one's attention to Christ or the saints by building a church or chapel on the spot. In a word, Christianity is a sacramental faith, and by that we mean we encounter Christ in the material world he has blessed by his redemption.

1 Thessalonians 4:14-18

Relatively new on the scene within the gamut of two thousand years of Christian tradition and biblical interpretation is the phenomenon known as "the rapture." The rapture's role in feeding the popular imagination with a false interpretation of the Last Judgment has had a great bearing on forming the view of demons, angels, and human behavior in dangerous ways.

The rapture is based on a wildly misguided reading of the text Saint Paul wrote to console the early believers in Thessaloniki. There is no record of its being a concern in the early church, and it has no resonance among Catholic, Orthodox, Armenian, non-Chalcedonian, Lutheran, Anglican, and most Protestant churches.

These people of Thessaloniki had become Christian and lived in the hope of the resurrection, but that hope also constituted a deep worry. What about their loved ones who had died, had never heard of Christ, and therefore had never been baptized? Would those who had predeceased them be saved? It certainly is a legitimate question whose answer has all sorts of ramifications. Paul's response, unfortunately, has become the flag around which gather the most extreme of American Christian fundamentalists, and because it figures into much of the current popular literature on life, death, angels, and demons, it is quoted here:

> For since we believe that Jesus died and rose again, even so, through Jesus, God will bring with him those who have died. For this we declare to you by the word of the Lord, that we who are alive, who are left until the coming of the Lord, will by no means precede those who have died. For the Lord himself, with a cry of command, with the archangel's call and with the sound of God's trumpet, will descend from heaven, and the dead in Christ will rise first. Then we who are alive, who are left, will be caught up in the clouds together with them to meet the Lord in the air; and so we will be with the Lord forever. Therefore encourage one another with these words. (1 Thess 4:14-18)

The operative verb in the discussion is "caught up," the translation of the Greek *harpázo*, meaning "to seize, steal, or carry away." Saint Paul uses it to describe the suddenness with which one will meet his or her judgment at the resurrection of the dead. When that moment comes, says Saint Paul, those still living will be seized and carried away to stand with the dead and meet the Lord. Although there is nothing in this passage from 1 Thessalonians that in any way suggests some kind of selection process whereby only some people are carried away into heaven, believers in the rapture hold that only the righteous will be included, and, of course, they themselves are the righteous.

It is difficult to find where and how one can reach such a conclusion about the rapture. It certainly does not come from anything else written in the New Testament, and it has no part of Christian Tradition. Perhaps the apocalyptic section in the gospels may have contributed to the confusion (Matt 24:3-44; Mark 13:1-37; Luke 21:6-36). These sections, however, speak about death in the face of persecution and say nothing about the judgment of anyone's deeds. In fact, a careful reading of the New Testament, especially the last judgment in Matthew, presents an entirely different scene.

Matthew and Paul are both speaking about the Last Judgment, but they see it and interpret it in two different ways. Matthew presents both the righteous and unrighteous simultaneously; moreover, no one among them can tell who is good and who is not; only Christ can distinguish the sheep from the goats (Matt 25:31-46). In 1 Thessalonians, Paul wants to emphasize that Christians will be reunited with their loved ones who have died before them, and that text, similar to the Matthean one, is inclusive in that all the living, good and bad, face judgment.

The greatest error in the fundamentalist interpretation, however, is the sweeping condemnation of the other. After dividing all the living into the good and bad, fundamentalism takes for itself the power of judgment that belongs to God alone. Furthermore, the assertion that some are saved and all others are lost to perdition goes against Christ's own teaching (Matt 7:1-2; Luke 6:37-38). The truth of the matter is that when the final trumpet sounds, Christ will judge, and all evidence indicates that his mercy is boundless and beyond human comprehension. The rapture as popularly conceived is egocentric and thus a false teaching and has no place among people of faith.

Revelation

Angels figure prominently within the book of Revelation. The opening verse of Revelation states that Jesus Christ has made the book's message known by "sending his angel to his servant John" (Rev 1:1b), and the writer reiterates the point in the last chapter with, "It is I, Jesus, who sent my angel to you with this testimony for the churches. I am the root and the descendant of David, the bright morning star" (22:16). While this particular angel makes Jesus' message known, there are approximately seventy-seven other occurrences of an angel or angels in Revelation, nearly four references per chapter.

The angels all have different functions, from pronouncing upcoming events to bringing predictions to completion. The angels in Revelation can be organized into four categories, with varied tasks for each: courtly, revelatory, guardian, and military. Some courtly angels worship the Lord,[6] while other angels in the court are agents of the divine plan.[7] Moreover, some of these agents that are apocalyptic at one point (15:1; 18:21)[8] will be eschatological later in the narrative (19:9; 21:9).[9] There is only one revelatory angel whose sole job is relating the message of the book to John of Patmos (1:1; 22:16). The guardian angels are not that numerous,[10] but the military angels are sufficient in number to defeat the forces of Satan (12:7, 9).[11]

The angel who bears the message from Christ in 1:1 must correct John of Patmos when the latter confuses this angel with Christ himself (22:8-9). The writer of Revelation must have had need to include such a correction for the readership of his day, a time that connected angels to the Godhead but that had not yet developed the theology to distinguish angelic beings from the resurrected Christ. This statement, from the Christian perspective, is one of the most salient points in the discussion about angels. Angels have no meaning apart from God's purposes. In both the Old and New Testaments, angels forward the divine agenda and draw all meaning for their existence from God. And those angels that are separate from God? In Scripture, they are the forces that try to confound God's plan, and Revelation gives us examples of them as well.

Revelation's Satanic Forces

No other book in the Bible gives us such a vivid picture of the devil and evil powers than Revelation. The terms used to portray these entities draw from a rich tradition of apocalyptic literature, of which Daniel is a prime example. Although separated by approximately three centuries, with allusions to two different eras, both Daniel[12] and Revelation[13] exhibit the same apocalyptic genre and similar vocabulary, even though the immediate referents of the vocabulary are entirely different.

Daniel is written within the context of the Seleucid kingdom, one of the major divisions of Alexander's empire, while Revelation is set well within the Roman Empire. Both use coded language when referring to these secular powers for fear of bloody retaliation at the hands of those same powers. The Seleucids for Daniel and the Romans for Revelation are manifestations of and agents for Satan's reign. Any interpretation of these two writings must always keep this point in mind in order to make sense of the text as well as not to fall into speculative, erroneous, and even dangerous conclusions.

The writers of Daniel and Revelation are clever in hiding the names of their oppressors within their respective texts—John of Patmos, the reputed writer of Revelation doubly so, for he uses some of the same language as in Daniel but differs in its application. The narrative for the book of Daniel is set in Babylon at the time of the exile under King Belshazzar, when in actual fact it was written when the Jews were under the thumb of the Seleucid Empire, whose king was Antiochus IV Epiphanes. References to Babylon are actually references to the Seleucids, and since Babylon was a major Persian conquest, and the Persians were the enemies of the Greeks, the Seleucids, if they ever got hold of the book of Daniel would never suspect its author or readers of treason.

In like vein, John of Patmos refers to Babylon when he means Rome in the book of Revelation. The Parthians, Rome's fearful enemy on it eastern border, came from the deserts of Mesopotamia. Rome too would never suspect that the term "Babylon" was a direct reference to Rome itself, and therefore the author and readers of Revelation would be beyond reproach should the Romans ever read the work.

The primary enemy in Revelation is the "beast," from the Greek term *therion*; all such references are found within Revelation 11–20. First mentioned by John of Patmos when he prophesies that it will climb out from the bottomless pit (11:7), the beast actually rises out of the sea in Revelation 13:1 where it is further described. An amalgamation of a leopard, a bear, and a lion, the beast is a monster-like creature that should not be confused with the dragon in Revelation 12. The dragon is Satan (12:9), while the beast represents and acts in the name of Satan (13:2, 4). Finally, the text states that the beast is a person who can be identified by the number 666 (13:18).

A purveyor of all things evil, this beastly person walks about with ten horns topped by ten diadems, having seven heads, and looking like a leopard with a bear's feet and a lion's mouth. For all of that, the most important feature for so many parties is that the beast carries the name of 666; it is the Antichrist.

The Antichrist is easy to identify. As does the Latin language, Hebrew and Greek use letters to write their numbers. In this verse, if the Greek letters are transliterated into Hebrew, we get the number 666, which also spells out *NronQrs* or *Nero(n) Caesar*, the initials of Nero Caesar, the Roman emperor who reigned from AD 60 to 68 and who was responsible for the deaths of many Christians, including Saints Peter and Paul. In addition, each of the digits in the number 666 is one less from the perfect and good number, seven. Thus, the community would understand that 666 is the antithesis of good and is, therefore, absolute evil. Although this number points to Nero, within the storyline the beast represents the city and Empire of Rome (13:1-10) and its emperor (13:11-18). This duplication of imagery emphasizes the depths of depravity and wickedness associated with Rome's earthly might.

Many are confused about the significance of the 144,000 redeemed people. The number 144,000 results from multiplying twelve by twelve thousand (14:1). Among the cultures affected by the Babylonian civilization, twelve is considered a perfectly complete and full number. The writer wishes to impress upon the reader the size of this gathering of persons; it is composed of completeness and perfection multiplied. Moreover, the text stipulates that each division comes from a respective tribe of ancient Israel, and it draws from the Christian Tradition in which each apostle represents one of Israel's twelve tribes. The 144,000, by leading the multitude, show the connection that Christianity and Judaism have with each other, for Christianity cannot be understood without relation to biblical Judaism. There is absolutely no basis for maintaining that the 144,000 is the sum total of all the people who will be saved from the creation of the world until today. Indeed, the book of Revelation implies that the 144,000 are the same as the "great multitude that no one could count" (7:9).

The difficulty for the reader of Revelation lies in the fact that its narrative line is not really a line at all; it is cyclical and spiral. Nor is the narrative clearly sequential or logical, with a certain cause always yielding the expected effect. So, for example, an earthquake levels a tenth of the city (read, imperial Rome). This destruction is followed by a warning of the impending third woe (11:13). Then comes the seventh trumpet blast, and instead of another cataclysm, the scene is one of a heavenly chorus praising the Lord for transforming this world into the eternal, heavenly realm (Rev 11:17-19). The third woe is never explicitly described as such in the book, though it is implied by the great battle in Revelation 12. For contemporary readers to hold Revelation to our Western, twenty-first-century expectations of a narrative sequence will inevitably lead to a dead end or, worse yet, an erroneous and dangerous conclusion. By using liturgical imagery of books, lampstands, vestments, choirs, and altars as well as references to the Roman Empire along with dramatic language, Revelation relates the history, theology, and focus of the Christian faith and the believer's life within it.

Throughout much of Revelation, a great many references employ words of sexual immorality, such as "whore" and "fornication." Such vocabulary reflects the OT understanding of idolatry. The prophets constantly accuse the people of abandoning the covenant and running after false gods, and they do so by using these same terms. The image relies on the common expression of the covenant as a spousal relationship between the Lord God as a faithful husband and the People Israel as a faithful wife. If the people turn to false gods of their neighbors, it is as if a woman has broken the marriage vows. When Revelation speaks of harlotry and sexual misconduct, therefore, it is drawing on the same metaphor. Those who put their trust and devotion in the Roman Empire are idolaters, with the various Roman emperors as idols and false gods.

The Apocalyptic Battle

At the end of Revelation 11, we are left with voices in heaven proclaiming, "The kingdom of the world has become the kingdom of our Lord and of his Messiah, and he will reign forever and ever" (11:15). The twenty-four elders join in saying that the reign of the Lord is about to begin. The very next chapter begins the great apocalyptic battle, which stands in contrast to the conclusion of Revelation 11. This contrast, however, provides an excellent description of Christian eschatology, which the combination of the woman, the dragon, and the action evoke.

We cannot easily identity the pregnant woman with the twelve-starred diadem (Rev 12:1-2). Scholars have seen her as Eve, Mary the Mother of God, and even the church. Most likely, she represents all three simultaneously. The child whom she births is Jesus Christ. The dragon is the devil or Satan. The

1,260 days in the desert (Rev 12:6) is a reprise of the number of days the two witnesses are given to prophesy (Rev 11:3). The number 1,260 itself is divisible by twelve, the basic unit of measurement of the Mesopotamian world. In both cases, readers must not take the number literally, and because it is not meant to be calculated, it cannot be. Rather, it explains a finite time within the plan of God.

The chapter gives a wonderful explanation of the Christian narrative as well as the Christian life. The enmity between Eve and the serpent (Gen 3:14-15) continues (Rev 12:4-5 ["dragon" = serpent]). Mary gives birth to Christ, and although threatened by Satanic powers, the divine Christ is not subject to the devil, and, in fact, Christ now sits at God's throne (Rev 12:5). This fact is made manifest in Jesus' earthly life, and that reign established by his earthly ministry continues until now. Mary is the mother of the church and, as a symbol of eschatological hope,[14] the church's role model (Rev 12:13-17). The church, then, continues to give birth to Christ within the world (recalling the witnesses of Rev 11:3), and just as Satan could not dominate Jesus in his earthly life and cannot do so now in his glorified one, so too will Satan not dominate Christ's church on earth. Nonetheless, Satan will threaten it and cause it temporary suffering.

The great battle between Michael and his host of angels against the dragon Satan along with his angelic followers demonstrates the eschatological situation; Christ rules even now, though we have not yet seen the fullness of his dominion. Michael and his army drive Satan from heaven to earth, and although the devil tries to undo the archangel's victory by flooding the woman and her child, the earth comes to the aid of the woman and swallows up the river (Rev 12:16). That the earth comes to the aid of the fleeing woman is a detail that underscores three very important points. First, the earth belongs to the Lord God. God created it and saw that it was good (Gen 1:1–2:3). Second, God confirms the earth's goodness by choosing to send his son to become incarnate in it and sealing that loving incarnation with his blood. The third point is an understanding implied rather than stated: because God-created earth is good, God will not destroy it, and Satan cannot.

With the dragon's abilities to conquer the world or hold God's people captive thus neutralized, this symbol of Satan now stands on the seashore to await the beast (whom we know to be Rome) to climb out from the depths and do diabolical deeds for its master. Revelation 12–13 stand at the heart of the book. In highly symbolic language they paint a picture of living the Christian life within the eschaton, a time in which Christ rules even while humankind has not yet seen the fullness of his reign. The eschaton is a period in which, despite the language of Revelation, people, times, and places cannot be organized exclusively into the two categories of God and Satan, black and white, good and evil. Rather, good and evil live side by side and often rub elbows; indeed, rather than being destroyed, most often evil can be converted to good, as the remaining chapters of Revelation demonstrate.

The Eschaton

Scholars have shown that the book of Revelation evidences both apocalyptic and eschatological sources. As a general rule, apocalyptic material describes natural and supernatural destruction and features cosmic battles between good and evil. Eschatological literature, on the other hand, while containing some apocalyptic elements, stresses the culmination of history in which there is a new creation and an end to all suffering.

While Revelation is widely known even in non-Christian circles, it is not the only book in the New Testament containing apocalyptic material. The Gospels of Matthew, Mark, and Luke have whole chapters describing the end of the world, which match in tone like passages in Revelation. The existence of this literature within various works of the New Testament as well as in certain books of the Old Testament[15] bears witness to the stress and fears that many of the Jewish and Christian faithful had during moments of persecution; such anxiety is an out-growth of chaos and evil. It is important to keep the historical contexts in mind when forming any kind of interpretation of biblical texts, especially with any apocalyptic literary genre found within those texts.

The respective apocalypses in Matthew, Mark, and Luke are situated before the passion narratives, when Jesus is about to undergo his suffering, death, and resurrection. Christ paints a picture in hair-raising detail in each, but he does so not to frighten his disciples but to give them hope and strength in the face of adversity. In addition, he says nothing about punishing anyone, a detail one should not overlook. Because Matthew elaborates in greater detail the eschatological themes inherent in all three synoptic accounts, examples from this gospel make these points clearer.

The parable of the wheat and weeds ends with the reapers gathering the weeds and throwing them into the fire (Matt 13:24-30). They do this only at harvest time lest the wheat be confused with the weeds. The meaning of the parable is nearly self-explanatory, yet Jesus, not leaving to chance what could be so erroneously interpreted, explains it for his disciples (Matt 13:36-43). The devil has sown evil on the land of God's creation with the result that good and bad will dwell alongside each other until the final days when the *angels*, acting as God's agents, will do the sorting. Humans are not to assume that they are to separate out those whom they regard as evil. Moreover, for humans to engage in such a task would be an act of disobedi-ence and, therefore, the work of Satan. Judging human souls is to be left in the hands of God. In approaching the other es-chatological passages, therefore, the reader must keep in mind the lesson of this parable.

Matthew's central apocalyptic passage (24:3-44), which has parallels in Mark and Luke, has many references to events, places, and people of the Roman world over two thousand years ago. In addition, much of the symbolic language, such as the sun and moon ceasing in their light and the stars falling from heaven (24:29) draws on much of the apocalyptic literature of the period and have no bearing on events today. For instance, the reference to the "desolating sacrilege" in Mark 13:14 can mean either the desecration of the Jerusalem temple by Antiochus IV Epiphanes in 167 BC, Pompey's violation of the temple's holy of holies in 63 BC, or the Roman conquest of Jerusalem in AD 70. It has no bearing on any event outside the intertestamental world.

Finally, there is the statement, "But about that day and hour no one knows, neither the angels of heaven, nor the Son, but only the Father" (Matt 24:36); Mark says something similar (13:32). If these very texts state that it is impossible for anyone but the Father to know when the end times will occur, we are left with the same conclusion we found in the parable of the weeds and wheat, that is, humans must not judge anyone, not even themselves. Calculating the end of the world is making such a judgment, for it implies that we know who is good and who is bad.

Matthew provides the only description of the Last Judgment among the four evangelists (25:31-46). It does not contain apocalyptic descriptors as much as it does eschatological ones. For example, the Son of Man comes with all his angels in glory, but the heavens do not fall, there are no earthquakes, and there certainly are no beasts or monsters. Even Satan is not mentioned. These verses, however, give us the clearest picture of what constitutes the case of our individual judgment: our loving concern for our neighbor or the lack thereof. The goats are damned (more correctly, damn themselves) because they are totally oblivious to the needs of those around them. The sheep are saved because they are so attuned to the suffering of others that they cannot imagine acting in any other way, hence, their question: "Lord, when was it that we saw you hungry and gave you food, or thirsty and gave you something to drink?" (Matt

25:37). Finally, we cannot lose sight of the fact that sheep and goats naturally separate themselves, yet Matthew's description indicates that the sheep and the goats cannot tell the difference between each other. The people of Jesus' day would have known this detail. The lesson is that we do not know who is who either, and, therefore, we cannot separate sheep from goats ourselves; doing so is in God's hands alone.

While Matthew does not include any earthquakes in this scene, he is the only evangelist to describe an earthquake at the death of Jesus (27:51-54) and to feature one at the resurrection (28:2). For Matthew, the end of the old order and the beginning of the new has already occurred at the death and resurrection of Jesus. The eschatological age has arrived, and we are living in it. True, this eschatological age is not yet in its fullness, but this paradox well presents the Christian life. Moreover, neither the damned nor the saved has a mark or a number.

All three Synoptics, most particularly Matthew, present the great dynamic tension that aptly demonstrates the Christian life. We live an eschatological life even now, as we await that age which has not yet fully come. The Last Judgment is based on how well we follow the example of Christ in feeding the hungry, clothing the naked, and working for righteousness and justice. Although we may not succeed in all our efforts, we need only try. Consequently, we cannot judge anyone, not even ourselves; our salvation is in Christ's merciful hands. We have proof of God's all-abiding mercy by the passion, death, and resurrection of Christ his Son.

By placing Revelation within the Great Tradition of the Gospel context, Christians throughout the ages have rightly concluded that faith and trust in the mercy of God form the foundational optic for interpreting the whole book of Revelation. While many would prefer to concentrate on the apocalyptic sections of Revelation, to do so is to focus on only one half of the story, and the misleading half at that. The complete picture comes into focus only with keeping in mind eschatological elements, particularly the establishment of the new and eternal Jerusalem with the ingathering of all peoples (Rev 21:3). Revelation 21–22 paint a glorious scene that Jesus expresses in John's gospel: "Indeed, God did not send the Son into the world to condemn the world, but in order that the world might be saved through him" (3:17).

Summary

We do not live in a dualistic universe in which good and evil are locked in an eternal battle whose outcome is unknown. Christ's victory over sin and death is eternal, and all humankind is invited to share in it. By asserting the incarnation and resurrection of Christ, Christianity has admitted to believing in the supernatural; furthermore, to believe in the triune God is to believe in the supernatural. To acknowledge that angels and demons exist, therefore, is logical and normal. Often, the activity of angels and demons will fall into the category of *paranormal*, a psychological term. While a great many of supernatural phenomena can be explained as psychological occurrences, not all of them can.

Any Christian discussion on the supernatural must reference the living Christian Tradition and Sacred Scripture. Tradition and Scripture have not only given us the vocabulary for such a discussion but also shaped our understanding of God, Satan, angels, and demons. They all factor into salvation history.

Nothing in Genesis links the serpent in the Garden to Satan or the devil; such identification has been read back into the text through the centuries, which is legitimate. In addition, angels as messengers are often confused with the Lord within the text itself. The alternation between the angel of the Lord and the Lord himself continues through Exodus. Exodus also stresses that the Lord God is in charge of the universe, and there are no credible competitors, and, indeed, this emphasis continues throughout the rest of the Pentateuch. The Pentateuch also contains legislation against fortune telling and necromancy, which comes into play in 1 Samuel.

In the Historical Books, we see the Israelites falling into idolatry by worshiping the named deities of the neighboring peoples. Whenever they do, bad things happen to them, and they return to the Lord God. Simultaneously, angels function as messengers answering the peoples' prayers, and unlike in Genesis, these angels are separate entities not to be confused with the Lord God. Stories about the idolatry of the Israelites surface again in 1 Kings; Elijah the Prophet becomes a strong voice against this apostasy and meets opposition from the foreigners with whom the Israelites have married, especially from the royal household. Because idolatry is unfaithfulness to the Lord God, the prophets consider it to be akin to fornication.

Tobit assigns certain tasks to certain angels and gives names to demons. The demons try to subvert the Lord's will, and the archangel Gabriel comes to Tobit's aid. Throughout the book, the demons are identified by their deceitful practices.

The book of Job features the first use of "Satan" as a proper noun; the term is derived from the Hebrew word for "adversary" and does not imply an evildoer. The Psalms display a wide array in their treatment of foreign gods; contemporary readers can see the faith development of the people move from monolatry to monotheism. The Lord God of Israel is the Lord of the universe. In addition, the worship of foreign gods becomes tied to evil and immoral practices.

Proverbs and the Wisdom of Solomon connect evildoing with death. On the other hand, righteousness brings forth life. Righteousness is victorious over evil, and when we engage in false worship, we place ourselves under the thralldom of death, as evidenced by the heinous practices tied to false worship, such as human sacrifice. True worship, because it is directed toward the Creator and not the creature, leads to true life.

The prophetic literature ties immoral practices to both idolatry and to the worship of demons. This combination leads to punishment and death. Furthermore, true worship of the Lord God must entail justice within the society. This addition to the prayer and liturgical life of the people highlights the life-giving attribute of the Lord God and the death-dealing nature of idol worship. As we move to the New Testament, the theology builds on these themes as it develops the lordship of Christ.

In the gospels we see Christ engaged in a cosmic battle with Satan. Every cure, healing, and exorcism asserts the Lord's reign and dominion over the cosmos he created. Despite the devil's attempts to usurp God's lordship, life and freedom in this world and in the next always triumph over sin, slavery, and death. Christ's victory is sealed by his passion, death, and resurrection.

The other New Testament writings, particularly Saint Paul's, reflect on Christ's salvific act and address the many questions that believers have concerning the redemption. Through the lens of the eternal life promised by Christ, Paul discusses the nature of good and evil and the new creation made possible by Christ and only by Christ.

For Christians the whole Bible concludes with the book of Revelation. This last work, known for its fiery metaphorical language and symbolically combative images, wrestles with the tensions between good and evil. Written for a community oppressed by imperial forces, Revelation concludes with an eschatological vision in which evil, sin, and death are defeated and all creation is transformed into the heavenly Jerusalem.

Conclusion

In the gospels, Christ's incarnation launches a cosmic battle with Satan. Suffering, sin, and death are part of the diabolical realm, which Christ combats in his ministry and, above all, by his passion, death, and resurrection. Demons are synonymous with unclean spirits, and the devil and Satan are one and the same being. The Bible concludes with a message of God's boundless mercy extended to everyone in the human race (Rev 22:17). Everyone in God's creation is predestined to be saved and is invited to share in Christ's ministry of salvation by being a disciple. No one is excluded for reasons of race, creed, gender, or sexuality. Taken in its fullness of the living Tradition, Sacred Scripture presents the essential truth that good reigns eternally and God's mercy endures forever.

PART 2

Angels

Chapter 5

Development of Angels
in the Christian Tradition

A long time exists between the descriptions of angels we read in the Bible and the angels dancing on Christmas trees, the cherubs holding up ornate cornices on buildings, and the pixies decorating greeting cards. Likewise, stories of angels today are told through DVDs, television shows, and movies, and they appear nothing like those in the biblical narrative. Just as there is an understanding of angels within the Christian tradition, there is a history of angels in the cultural imagination. When the culture was predominantly and professedly Christian, angel stories were read one way, and now that, in the West at least, the culture is multifaceted and multidimensional, angel stories are read in another.[1]

The hierarchy of angels, the careers of the more famous names in the heavenly choir, and the job descriptions of guardian angels arise from the biblical narrative and find meaning within the Christian context as well as, with certain variation, within the Jewish one. The secular understanding adopts some of the Jewish and Christian contexts but ultimately makes a substantial departure from them.

What an Angel Is and Is Not

Discussions about angels can sometimes lead to a certain deal of confusion, which the popular culture does little to clarify. To set the record straight, we should keep in mind these details: God created the angels. They are purely spiritual beings who do not have physical bodies and will never have them. They are not born, and they do not die. They do not have souls. They are living entities in their own right. Above all, upon death, human beings enter eternal life; they do not become angels. This last point is important because all too often people mix human salvation with the angelic existence, which causes problems in understanding our lives here on earth.

As we have seen, there is no biblical account revealing God's creation of the angelic order. The closest reference we have is Genesis 6:4, "The Nephilim were on the earth in those days—and also afterward—when the sons of God went in to the daughters of humans, who bore children to them. These were the heroes that were of old, warriors of renown." What we know and believe about angels comes from extrabiblical sources, particularly I and II Enoch and other pseudepigraphic works. Later authors, such as Dante and Milton, elaborated and popularized these stories to the point that most people assume that facts about angels come from the biblical record. Very little does come from Scripture, however. Nonetheless, when the biblical narrative is combined with the extrabiblical sources, we are able to piece together a consistent understanding if not always a logically clear one.

The Hierarchy of Angels

The most famous angels, by all accounts, would have to be Saints Michael, Gabriel, and Raphael. Throughout the ages, both the masculine and feminine forms of their names have been bestowed on newly born children by countless parents. Churches, mountains, abbeys, shrines bear the name "Michael." "Raphael" is associated with places and occupations dealing with the sick and healing, while Gabriel is found on every painting dealing with the incarnation as well as the call to judgment. Indeed, at least from a cultural perspective, these angels, or more correctly, archangels, represent the classic representation of the heavenly being.

Little in the Old and New Testaments furnishes the material for stories associated with the archangels. Michael as a heavenly being first surfaces in Daniel (10:13, 21; 12:1) and is described as a chief prince who contends with the princes of Persia. Michael reappears in Jude (1:9) and in Revelation (12:7). We read of Gabriel in Daniel (8:16; 9:21), but he is better known for proclaiming to Mary that, with her consent, she is to be the mother of God (Luke 1:19, 26). The book of Tobit is the source of Raphael's fame. Appearing, reappearing, and assisting throughout the book, Raphael finally identifies himself by declaring, "I am Raphael, one of the seven angels who stand ready and enter before the glory of the Lord" (Tob 12:15).

This last statement by Raphael clues the reader to the fact that there are actually seven angels at the ready before the throne of the Lord, and from this verse develops the tradition of the archangels. Though we do not hear much about the four others, the Tradition supplies us their names (see p. 67 below). The archangels are, however, one type of angel within the lowest tier of angels; there are another two tiers above them.

It should be clear at this point that *angelology*, the proper name for the study of angels, is more varied and historical than one might commonly expect; questions we ask about angels are in many ways no different from those posed by the ancient writers. The Jewish and Christian biblical canons have many references to angels, but they do not describe them or relate much about them. For any elaborate narratives of angels, we must go to the apocryphal, deuterocanonical, or pseudepi-graphic works,[2] which flourished during the intertestamental era. In fact, these works were the sources for several ancient writers who classified many of the angels in ways we still use. Especially in the pseudepigraphic works, it was not uncommon for authors to use pseudonyms based on biblical personages, and it was one such individual who formulated a schema categorizing most of the angels with which we are familiar today.

Pseudo-Dionysius

In the Acts of the Apostles, Paul goes to Athens and finds himself preaching in the Areopagus, an area located next to the Acropolis and, at different times in history, the place of the law courts and the Athenian Council. His efforts to gain converts to the Way are nearly fruitless, but one person joins Paul, Dionysius the Areopagite (Acts 17:18-34). As the name would indicate, Dionysius was no doubt a member of Athens' intellectual elite. Since he was both an Athenian scholar and a Christian convert, an anonymous author around AD 500 used his name to pen in Greek a vision titled the *Celestial Hierarchy*. In the middle of the ninth century, the *Celestial Hierarchy* was translated into Latin, which spread Dionysius's name and writings to the West. So accepted was the *Celestial Hierarchy* that it formed the basic taxonomy for the church's understanding of angels for centuries.

No one questioned the authenticity of the *Celestial Hierarchy* until Lorenzo Valla, the great Italian Renaissance scholar. Using textual criticism, Valla gained both fame and notoriety by revealing the Donation of Constantine to be a hoax.[3] He applied like methods to the *Celestial Hierarchy* and demonstrated that it dates from between AD 400 and 500—much too late to come from the hand of one of Saint Paul's celebrated converts. From this time forward, "Dionysius" has been known as "Pseudo-Dionysius." Despite the bogus origins of the *Celestial Hierar-*

chy, its content has remained the reference point of angels until today, at least as far as it applies to nomenclature. In addition, Pope Gregory the Great (ca. 540–604) also presents a similar hierarchical angelic arrangement in his writings.[4]

Pseudo-Dionysius organizes angels into three major tiers of three choirs each. Throughout history, this schema held sway, despite rearranging by some.[5] Some of the greatest theologians, such as Aquinas, Bonaventure, and Peter Lombard, stand upon the foundation of Pseudo-Dionysius's *Celestial Hierarchy*. That they do opens a provocative question, however. If angelology is based on a spurious vision to a person, whom we must name Pseudo-Dionysius for his false claims, does not everything written about angels since the fifth century dissolve into nonsense? Not exactly.

To be sure, the *Celestial Hierarchy* is pure fantasy and conjecture, but its strength does not rely on whether someone had such a vision of heaven with its attendant angels. As we have seen from the descriptions and actions of angels in the Bible, these heavenly messengers are interpreted as manifestations of divine attributes; where God's will and agency ends and where an angelic being begins is a gray zone. Notwithstanding the artifice of the *Celestial Harmony*, it describes well a theology of how the Godhead and angels operate in the universe, and its literary invention has served a noble purpose. It has codified and organized divine initiative and action throughout salvation history. Moreover, while it may appear that Pseudo-Dionysius fabricated a clever fantasy, it arose from a spiritual worldview of his time; his description is not baseless.

There are passages in Scripture, most notably from Saint Paul, that describe different levels of heaven and presence of angels. When we read these references within the context of the Hellenistic world from which Sacred Scripture arises, the *Celestial Hierarchy* is not all that original; in fact, one might even call it derivative of everything people of the fifth century more or less understood about angels.[6] Pseudo-Dionysius simply systematizes it. Since the *Celestial Hierarchy* has had such an influence on Christian civilization's concept and understanding of angels, we would do well to continue to use its basic outline as we speak about the role of angels today.

First Hierarchy
- seraphim
- cherubim
- thrones

Second Hierarchy
- dominions
- virtues
- powers

Third Hierarchy
- principalities
- archangels
- angels

First Hierarchy

The name *seraph* comes from the Hebrew word for "burning," and in all of Scripture, it surfaces only in Isaiah 6:2 and 6:6 in its plural form, "seraphim" or "seraphs" (depending on the version of the biblical translation). In this passage, Isaiah has a vision in the temple in which he sees the throne of the Lord. The account reads, "Seraphs were in attendance above him; each had six wings: with two they covered their faces, and with two they covered their feet, and with two they flew. And one called to another and said: 'Holy, holy, holy is the Lord of hosts; the whole earth is full of his glory' " (Isa 6:2-3). The seraphs' six wings combined with their call of "Holy, holy, holy" situates them squarely before the throne of God where their only job is to sing eternal praise to the Lord.

The role of cherubs or cherubim is also defined in Scripture in a good many references. "Cherub" itself means "great and mighty." They guard the tree of life once Adam and Eve are driven from the garden, the logic being that proximity to the Lord is participation in divine knowledge, a privilege that the primordial couple forfeited by their sin. In other books of the Bible, particularly Exodus, 1 Kings, and 1 and 2 Chronicles, the cherubim are carved figures adorning the ark of the covenant and the tabernacle; as beings full of knowledge and wisdom, they represent eternal contemplation of the divine presence. In Ezekiel, however, the prophet's vision furnishes nearly all the references to the cherubim.[7]

While it is difficult to form an image of what the cherubim really look like, their duty is to support the Lord on his throne: "Give ear, O Shepherd of Israel, you who lead Joseph like a flock! You who are enthroned upon the cherubim, shine forth before Ephraim and Benjamin and Manasseh. Stir up your might, and come to save us!" (Ps 80:1-2). Moreover, as the glory of the Lord moves in and out of various places, the cherubim carry him on their wings, as for example, "He rode on a cherub, and flew; he came swiftly upon the wings of the wind" (Ps 18:10).

Second Hierarchy

The writings of Saint Paul mention nearly all the next five ranks of heavenly beings at some point: thrones, dominions, virtues, powers, and principalities[8] (Rom 8:38; Eph 1:21; 3:10; Col 1:16; 2:10). As we see, these ranks encapsulate the last rung of the first hierarchy, all of the second, and the first rung of the third. Throughout the Christian Tradition, they do not receive nearly as much treatment at the hands of theologians as do the seraphim, cherubim, archangels, and angels.[9] Yet, the second hierarchy of dominions, virtues, and powers are agents of the

Lord, and they oversee, govern, and guide the functioning of the universe.

Third Hierarchy

Throughout history, discussions about angels have dealt predominantly with the intersection where people and angels meet. A look at the shelves in any religion section of contemporary bookstores or libraries will show countless works on angels. These books are a genre in their own right with stories following a predictable pattern and variation: A person is in serious if not life-threatening trouble, someone arrives in the nick of time and deflects the danger, the person turns around to thank the individual who has since disappeared without a trace and with no one else seeing the rescuer. Alternately, a person comes along, sees a person in dire need, assists the one in trouble, turns away for a second only to discover that the one requiring assistance has vanished.

According to the *Celestial Hierarchy*, angels of this type belong to the lowest tier, the one occupied by principalities, archangels, and angels. Indeed, mention of the ministries of the heavenly beings in the first and second hierarchies is scant when compared to the stories and devotion dedicated to the third. This fact is indicative of the incarnational and sacramental nature of Christianity. The principalities, archangels, and angels deal with human affairs and express the divine love emanating from the Creator toward his creation. It is a closeness engendered by the incarnation, passion, death, and resurrection of the Father's only begotten son, Jesus Christ.

Principalities. In the tradition of Christianity, Principalities watch over the human realm by inspiring good governance for the nations and kingdoms of the world; this stress on just and harmonious rule led to their being associated with divine providence.[10] In art, they are generally depicted wearing a crown and carrying a scepter.

Archangels. The term "archangel" occurs only in 1 Thessalonians 4:16 and Jude 1:9, yet this rank is the only one that has proper names associated with it. The major traditions of Christianity, both East and West, agree that there are seven archangels, though the best known and most popular are Michael, Gabriel, and Raphael. Raphael is disputed by some Protestant churches because he appears only in the deuterocanonical book of Tobit. Uriel is sometimes seen in various commentaries, but because the name occurs in a book that is seen as noncanonical in the West (4 Esdras), references to him eventually diminish. Likewise, scholars from early Christianity through the late Middle Ages treat Phanuel, Zarachiel, and Simiel sparingly, if at all, with these names occurring mostly in popular stories and legends.

Roman/Anglican	Lutheran	Reformed Protestant	Greek
Michael	Michael	Michael	Michael
Gabriel	Gabriel	Gabriel	Gabriel
Raphael	Raphael	———	Raphael
(Uriel)	———	———	Uriel
(Phanuel)	———	———	Sealtiel
(Zarachiel)	———	———	Jegudiel
(Simiel)	———	———	Barachiel
			Jeremiel (sometimes)

In dealing with the topic of archangels, we really mean the top three: Michael, Gabriel, and Raphael. The name of each of them is Hebrew in origin, and it establishes their function in creation. Michael means "One who is like God"; Gabriel, "Strength of God"; and Raphael, "Medicine of God."

While three of the archangels have prominence in Christian lore, Michael by far is the most popular. Cited first in the book of Daniel, Michael is called the "prince" of the angels who fights on Israel's behalf (Dan 10:13, 21; 12:1). Revelation shows

Michael battling and eventually defeating the dragon (12:7). Because the church considers herself the spiritual descendant of Israel, starting in the Middle Ages, Michael becomes the patron of holy places, churches, monasteries, kingdoms, and nations throughout the Christian world, and he is usually depicted with an upraised sword ready to stab Satan upon whose neck he is standing.[11]

Gabriel is mentioned four times in the Bible. He appears to Daniel in a vision (Dan 8:16; 9:21) and plays a major role in the infancy narratives of Luke's gospel. In the latter, Gabriel comes first to Zachariah to inform him that Elizabeth is pregnant (Luke 1:11-20). More famously, Gabriel appears to Mary and announces that she is to be the mother of God's son, Jesus (Luke 1:26-38). Despite the fact that the name Gabriel is never associated with blowing the trumpet on the last day, tradition has assigned the task to this archangel, no doubt based on the record of his announcing to earth the judgments of heaven.

The name of the archangel, Raphael, surfaces only in the book of Tobit, and because Tobit is a deuterocanonical work, some Protestant churches do not include Raphael among the archangels. In chapter 11 of the book, Raphael explains to Tobias, the son of Tobit, how to apply the fish's gall to his father in order to cure him of his blindness. This passage is responsible for making healing Raphael's primary attribute.

Angels. In most discussions about angels, the ultimate question centers on their role in our human lives. People would not be all that concerned about angels were it not for the fact that the Christian Tradition in particular but other traditions as well possess stories of individuals being rescued from some ill fate through the intercession of an angel. Alternatively, a person may have experienced some kind of beatific encounter or revelation through what is believed to be an angel. No matter how one describes the situation, the topic is an interaction with one's guardian angel.

The belief in guardian angels has both scriptural and non-Christian roots.[12] When Jesus speaks to the disciples about the blessedness of little children, he concludes, "Take care that you do not despise one of these little ones; for, I tell you, in heaven their angels continually see the face of my Father in heaven" (Matt 18:10). The idea that everyone has an angel watching over her is corroborated by the scene of Peter's escape in the Acts of the Apostles: "[I]nstead of opening the gate, she ran in and announced that Peter was standing at the gate. They said to her, 'You are out of your mind!' But she insisted that it was so. They said, 'It is his angel'" (Acts 12:14-15). Moreover, Tobit, not knowing that the traveling companion is actually the archangel Raphael, calls out to his son, "Son, prepare supplies for the journey and set out with your brother. May God in heaven bring you safely there and return you in good health to me; and may his angel, my son, accompany you both for your safety" (Tob 5:17). Along with these biblical references, influence from the ancient Greek notion that an individual had a personal spirit, either good or bad, attached to him also contributes to the idea of a guardian angel.[13]

For every story attributing to a guardian angel rescue from physical harm or danger, there are dozens in which injury or death come with no angel arriving to help the victim. Questions of why and how rightfully challenge believers. Simply, there is no answer. Rather, these situations cast the questions into a broader light. The Christian faith does not promise exemption from the laws of nature or from all suffering, but it does promise hope for a resurrected life free of pain and death beyond the present. There is a promise of such a life in the future that affects how one sees and lives one's life now. On this basis, the role of a guardian angel is more nuanced, for in all things and at all times the guardian angels manifest the providential hand of the Lord.

The foundational point for any interpretation of all angels, including guardian angels, is their relation to Christ. As we have seen with Sacred Scripture's treatment of angels, these heavenly beings are agents of the glory, strength, love, and care of the triune God toward God's creation. Any deed attributed to a guardian angel ultimately must be seen as originating in Christ, for guardian angels are expressions of grace.

While angels function to protect one from physical harm on earth, their primary purpose is to offer spiritual assistance when an individual faces temptation or demonic assaults, particularly at death. Such an understanding, however, raises the issue of free will. If a person commits an immoral or sinful act, what does it say about that person's culpability if it has resulted from the influence of an evil spirit? Furthermore, what does it say about the salvific power of Christ if one of his guardian angels could not thwart the designs of a demon?

One of the most important tenets of Christian theology is that no force can overcome free will.[14] On this basis, we really cannot blame our sinful behavior on a demon, nor can we say that we are mere automatons at the behest of a troupe of guardian angels. In our life experiences, we must deal with truth and deception every day and make decisions accordingly. It is not altogether different as we face the spiritual world. If a guardian angel is a supernatural being expressing God's grace, we should cooperate with that grace to the degree we are able in light of our limitations, but we are not obliged to.

That every human being has a personal guardian angel, according to the Christian Tradition, in no way diminishes Christ's role as savior of the universe. While it may seem that such a detail as guardian angels could lead one to dismiss the need for Christ and his redemption, an angel's singular attachment to an individual actually does the opposite: It makes the promises of Christ personal, even as those promises are universal and are made to the whole of creation. The ministry of the angels is not independent of the Lord God's supreme reign over the universe. The angels' involvement with the world is yet another way we experience Christ's ministry.

Chapter 6

Angels and Christ's Ministry: A Theology

The biblical story for Christians is Christ's triumph as Lord of the universe, and his ongoing involvement with creation through the sacraments. Indeed, the church is a sacrament. If angels are the expressions of Christ's grace, then it is only logical that they be associated in some way with the sacraments. At least that is how piety and art have dealt with angels through the ages.[1] This is to say that Christ is present in the sacraments, and with Christ's presence come the divine glory and love. Where there are divine glory and love, there are angels. In addition, the Bible, particularly the New Testament, shows angels at critical points in Christ's life, passion, and resurrection, and because Christians have considered themselves as disciples of Christ, it has become a natural step for angels to be present in major events of their Christian lives as well.

We have seen how the Bible presents the work of angels in the story of salvation. Angels play a prominent role in the events surrounding the birth of Christ. Not only does Joseph decide to wed Mary on the word of an angel (Matt 1:20-24), but through the intervention of an angel, the child Jesus is saved from Herod's massacre, and when danger passes, an angel calls to Joseph to return to Israel (Matt 2:13.19). In Luke's gospel, the angel Gabriel appears to Zechariah to announce the birth of John the Baptist (1:19) and to Mary to ask her to be the mother of God's son (1:26-38). From these instances, particularly from Luke, because the angel Gabriel is named and because the story is about Mary, the veneration of the angels becomes associated with salvation, and that veneration becomes tightly bound with devotion to Mary.[2] Arguably, the most popular prayer among Roman Catholics is the Hail Mary, the first half of which is quoted nearly verbatim from Luke 1:28-31. In the medieval period this prayer was elaborated by interposing between verses of the Hail Mary, Mary's response to Gabriel's announcement, a text also largely from Luke. The result has been the *Angelus*, which church bells still ring out at noon and six o'clock in the evening.

In Jesus' battle against the Evil One, angels are present. Just after Jesus' baptism, Matthew and Mark relate that he was cast into the desert to be tempted by the devil for forty days, with angels ministering to him there in the midst of it all. Thus, in the early church, angels become associated with aiding humankind against attacks of the devil, and exorcism becomes part of the baptismal rite. Moreover, because guardian angels are with a person for his or her whole life, the understanding arose that this angel became attached to the individual at baptism, and what better time? For if Christ himself had to deal with Satan after his baptism, so would we after ours.

Angels and the Holy Spirit

Angels announce the resurrection to Mary Magdalene and the others in Matthew 28:1-7 and John 20:11-15.[3] These spiritual beings are so closely associated with the resurrected Christ that in the prayer and development of the Tradition, they became associated with the sacraments. Let there be no mistake, however: The Holy Spirit, the third person in the Trinity, is the Intercessor and Paraclete. The Holy Spirit is not an angel, and angels are not manifestations of the Holy Spirit.

Angels are not causal; they are circumstantial. That is to say that the angels are part of the sacramental encounter, but they do not bring it into being. Christ, the Son of God, is the sacrament, and it is through Holy Spirit's action or intercession within the faith community that makes him present to us. We in turn gain access to Christ through our baptism into that same faith community. The presence of angels at the celebration of Christian sacraments is a natural conclusion, then. If they are part of the glory of heaven above, they witness that glory when it is present on earth below. In the sacraments we participate in the divine presence, and the angels are celebrating as well. In such good company, our intention to worship Christ and participate in his ministry can only have good results.

Humans and Angels

When the celebration of the Mass turns to the preface, the priest comes to the line enjoining those present to sing the Holy, Holy, Holy; the text reads the following or its equivalent: "And so we join the angels and saints in proclaiming your glory." It is a line that situates two separate orders of creation, the angelic and the human, within the whole order of creation by connecting the two in a way above and beyond the help and assistance that archangels and guardians have given humankind throughout salvation history. This connection is all part of Christ's redemption of all creation.

The Christian belief and claim is that Christ is the Lord of the universe; we see that understanding originating in the gospels and proclaimed by Paul; subsequent church councils have also declared it through creedal statements. The lordship is one of love, a love of such power and authority that it can conquer all hatred and violence. It is an unselfish love that can unify while still respecting the difference and uniqueness of everything that that love has created, and the sacramental life of the church is the way in which the church participates in that love. The call to all the baptized is not to forget that Christ is the center of church, and we are to worship him, not our own notions or opinions of how things should be within the church.

To be sure, the love of God knows no limit, and Christ's love extends to all humankind whether or not one is a baptized Christian. Baptism, however, opens one to participate in the full communion of Christ's love. The sacrament of communion is the Eucharist, and it is in the Eucharist that human action and prayer meet with divine love and grace in a way unlike any other, even as these components can meet in other venues and circumstances. So, what does the Eucharist have to do with angels? Within the great liturgical traditions of East and West, the Christian eucharistic liturgy is constructed on two axes, one vertical and the other horizontal. Human beings and all creation reach up to God along the vertical axis, while human beings reach out to each other as well as all creation along the horizontal axis.

The Vertical Axis

The book of Revelation is a model for the mind-set of the sacred liturgy. Its chapters are full of heavenly beings surrounding the throne of God offering continuous praise and song. There are readings from books, vestments, processions, choral anthems, dynamic tensions between the world we live in and the world yet to come, and, above all, there is the ingathering into the kingdom of all creation at the end of time (Rev 21:24-27).

We have seen how Pseudo-Dionysius has arranged all these heavenly creatures into three hierarchies, each with three ranks of angels. All together, the hierarchies comprise what has come to be called the *heavenly choir of angels*. Christ instituted the Eucharist during his earthly ministry; through it, he shares his divine life with us so that we can enter into that life. If we enter his divine life, then we stand alongside the heavenly powers in offering praise to the triune God. Elements within our celebration of the liturgy make this point evident.

The first Christmas hymn is sung by the angels who proclaim the Christ Child's birth to the shepherds (Luke 2:14). This angelic hymn has not only become the basis of the Gloria in Christian worship but also given birth to the whole tradition of Christmas carols, for, as the reasoning goes, if the angels sing, so should we. The *Sanctus* or Holy, Holy, Holy during the celebration of the Eucharist is a hymn, rendered by the whole choir of angels singing before God and his throne, and it is based on Isaiah 6:3 as well as Revelation 4:8; Christians participate in it along with the angels every time they worship at the Liturgy of the Eucharist.

Sometimes parts of the liturgy are an amalgamation of different biblical verses. For example, the book of Revelation refers to Christ as the "slaughtered Lamb" (5:6, 12; 13:8), and the phrase "Lamb of God" was evidently in use in the early church, as seen in John's gospel (1:29, 36). In Revelation, we read, "I heard the voice of many angels surrounding the throne and the living creatures and the elders; they numbered myriads of myriads and thousands of thousands, singing with full voice, 'Worthy is the Lamb that was slaughtered to receive power and wealth and wisdom and might and honor and glory and blessing!'" (5:11-12). This biblical image appears in the liturgy as the *Agnus Dei*, or Lamb of God, sung just before communion.

Similarly, in the Christian monastic tradition, one of the reasons monks and nuns gather up to eight or more times a day for communal prayer is to imitate the heavenly choir in ceaselessly singing praise to God; in fact, they sing for us as well. Because it is impossible to fulfill such a task and still do the work necessary for survival, over the centuries the ceaseless prayer has been divided into two hinges: Lauds or Morning Prayer to open the day and Vespers or Evening Prayer to close it. The other times occur at roughly three-hour intervals between these two. It should be said, however, that the great abbey of Cluny during the eleventh and twelfth centuries had so many monks that it constructed a rotation so that there was a choir in the church singing psalms and other prayers twenty-four hours a day.

The Horizontal Axis

The foundation of Christianity is Christ's incarnation; the Son of God has taken on human flesh. From that moment, creation became not only holy and sacred but also saved and redeemed.[4] As Jesus proclaims over and over again throughout the gospels, believers must love both God and neighbor, and these two components cannot and must not be separated.[5]

Again, we can see this axis in play during the Liturgy of the Eucharist. At the opening rite, worshipers call to mind their sins, and these sins are against God and neighbor. We attend to the horizontal axis through the various parts of the liturgy. In addition to the priest who serves the community, members of the community itself engage in different ministries such as lectors, altar servers, musicians, greeters, and bread and cup ministers in order to serve the rest of the worshiping body. At the preparation of the gifts, there is a collection for the needs of the assembly and for those suffering in the world.

What takes place within the liturgy must have bearing on the world outside the liturgy. For this reason, a Christian community or parish will help stock local food shelves, send people to visit the sick and homebound, and sponsor groups to assist areas ravaged by floods or suffering chronic poverty. Indeed, Catholic Relief Services has more offices in more countries and distributes more aid to trouble spots the world over than does the United Nations! A theology of angels and participation in liturgy mean very, very little unless they excite, lead, and direct us all to be disciples of Christ. We respect Christ and show our gratitude for his salvation when we follow his example here on earth by building the kingdom his passion, death, and resurrection have brought about.

Eschatology or the Kingdom of God

Placing both the vertical and horizontal axes within the context of the angels furthers the coming of the kingdom of God. A question that often surfaces is whether we are living in the kingdom of God here and now, or whether we will enter the kingdom of God when we die. The question is also sometimes referred to as a present or future eschatology.[6] If Christ already has come, lived, died, and risen among us, does this not mean that he has already ushered in the kingdom of God? On the other hand, if we look around, there is a lot in the world that would hardly qualify as an attribute of the kingdom of God.

Among the evangelists, John writes as if all the baptized are now living in the kingdom of God, whereas Matthew, Mark, and Luke take the view that the kingdom of God will come in the future, on the last day. The answer is that the kingdom of God is both. We are living even now in the kingdom of God that has not yet come to its full fruition. The vertical and horizontal dimensions of Christian liturgy keep the role of the angels in clear focus: angels are integral to the kingdom of God now and yet to come. We have seen how angels have a part in the biblical tradition. They bring messages to the people as well as lead and protect them. We see them performing their functions in both the Old and New Testaments. Furthermore, their work continues within the life of the church through their presence at the sacraments, their role of praise at the liturgy, and their guardianship of us. As created beings separate from humans, angels are the agents and manifestations of God's glory and grace, a glory and grace that can never be independent of the Trinity. In fact, without God, there can be no angels.

People become interested in angels because they, people, have concerns about the great beyond or the afterlife. Everyone wants to know what lies after this brief earthly existence of ours. For the Christian, this question finds its answer in life with Christ. Okay, but what does that mean? Does living a life in Christ mean that we become angels? Does it mean we will find ourselves as an inhabitant in one of the three hierarchies, and, if so, what are we supposed to do with all that time on our hands once the world has ended? Sing endless praises to God? The fact is that we do not become angels; angels are a separate order of creation. They are created as angels, and we are created as humans. Inasmuch as we will participate in the heavenly choir, how we participate depends on the kind of being we are to be.

If any of us were asked what happens to us when we die, most Christians would most likely answer that our bodies decay, but our souls go on living forever. It is an understandable response—after all, we have cemeteries and we have seen skeletons—but it is not really accurate. To be sure, we have souls that do not die. The soul, however, is not the issue; the issue is the body. In the Nicene Creed, Christians say, "I believe in . . . the resurrection of the body." How does a belief in the resurrection of the body harmonize with the corpse in the coffin? Here we enter one of the greatest Christian mysteries: eternal life and the resurrection of the body.

When Scripture employs the term "soul," it does so with the Hebrew understanding of "life," "personality," "being," and "selfhood," and this understanding holds throughout those books of the Bible written in Greek, such as the Greek Old Testament or Septuagint and the entire New Testament. Confusion has entered in with the Greek word for soul, *psyche*, which is overladen with Greek philosophical constructs, mostly from Stoicism. In this case, "soul" is defined in opposition to the body. Because the body experiences pain and pleasure, grows old, dies, and decays, it is bad. The soul, on the other hand, stands above pain and pleasure and never ages, let alone dies and decays. Therefore, the soul is good. For various reasons, many of them having to do with Hellenistic culture in which the early church found herself when she was defining her beliefs, much of the Greek view of the soul has permeated the Christian understanding of life and death. The result is that most Christians believe the two trajectories of eternal life and immortal soul simultaneously without ever really eschewing one for the other. Unfortunately, *eternal life* has not always received the attention it deserves.

Chapter 7

Souls: Immortality or Eternal Life?

In the history of thought of both East and West, immortality has taken on many forms. The one common characteristic of them all is that the spark or life principle of one's existence, often called the "soul," however it is defined—intelligence, consciousness, bloodline—somehow continues after death.

Among the Stoics[1] and their followers, for instance, there was a belief in astral immortality in which, upon death, the souls of the just (and the just meant the well-educated class of men; slaves and women were outside the caste) became stars. Additionally, other traditions and cultures at various times and even today have believed in reincarnation. In this system, the soul inhabits every living thing. When that plant, insect, or animal dies, the soul moves to another living thing, and thus on and on through all eternity. A variation of the reincarnation pattern is that, depending on how justly one lives in one particular form of life, one will either progress to a higher form, such as a plant to an invertebrate, to a mammal, and to a human, or regress to a lower form and go in the opposite direction. The goal in this system is to become so righteous and just that one will merit a life of eternal bliss.[2] Some other concepts of immortality maintain that we live on in our descendants, who in turn will venerate their ancestors, such as in Confucianism. There are those who hold that everyone's life force is part of the universe. To die is to return to that great life force, popularly called the "Ground of Being," and somehow live on in all and various forms of life.

As good as immortality in all its forms may be, it is not the promise that Christ holds out to the world. In addition, and I speak personally here, I find them so lacking in major ways. Astral immortality offers nothing but a bleak existence. Even if it were to democratize itself and allow for women and the underclass, who defines the standards used to measure just and righteous behavior? The upper classes with their rigged privileges? Reincarnation is hopelessly pessimistic. One life has enough challenges; I do not want to do it again and again. More troubling is what reincarnation does to my relationships. Do all the people I love in one life (assuming that I can at least stay on the human plane for a good piece of eternity) amount to nothing? Are one's mother, father, brothers, sisters, spouse, children, friends, and all other loved ones and acquaintances simply coincidences for twenty, forty, sixty, or ninety years, never to be seen or heard of again? At least living on in my ancestors respects the beauty and strength of relationships, but what happens when a family line dies out or is destroyed in some catastrophe? Finally, returning to the life force of the universe runs into the same problem as reincarnation.

In Christianity, love is the reason, the means, and the end of life. God is love, and love is life's driving force. God has created out of love, has sent his son into the world out of love, and in the end that Love and all that Love has loved return to the Creator to live eternally.

Eternal Life

Christ does not speak about immortality; he talks about eternal life and the salvation of the world.

The New Testament phrase "eternal life" appears in all four gospels, though mostly in John, and also in Acts and several of the letters.[3] When it is read with the Hebrew concept of *soul* in mind, the providential destiny of the Christian life comes into clear focus. Our total beings, our lives, our selfhood, our personalities will have eternal life. The resurrection accounts in the gospels tell us what this will be like as well as what it will not be like.

Matthew, Mark, Luke, and John all record Jesus' resurrection, yet these four books have different versions of exactly what happens on that first day of the week. Despite the differences, there are two constants running through all of them: the first, Mary Magdalene sees the empty tomb; and the second, Jesus rises bodily from the dead. It was not a spirit; it was his body.[4]

That Jesus' body is not in the tomb stands as one point confirming that what the disciples are seeing is not a spirit. Early deniers of the resurrection counter that his followers stole his body, but Matthew acknowledges the charge and argues against the accusation. Moreover, the resurrection texts mention that the burial shrouds are neatly folded. Grave robbers would not have unbound the body before running off with it. The real proof comes when people actually see the risen Christ, but even this experience is fraught with problems. In every account, the disciples see Jesus, but they do not know who he is. Yet, when he speaks or performs some action, they then recognize him. This simultaneous movement of nonrecognition and recognition tells us much about the resurrection of the body and eternal life, for what has happened to Jesus will happen to us.

We must keep in mind that Jesus is raised as a glorified body. Paradoxically, his is the same body people see in his earthly ministry, only different. There is no telling what that difference is except the gospel accounts present him functioning as a normal person while appearing and disappearing. At one point, Christ explicitly states, " 'Look at my hands and my feet; see that it is I myself. Touch me and see; for a ghost does not have flesh and bones as you see that I have.' And when he had said this, he showed them his hands and his feet. While in their joy they were disbelieving and still wondering, he said to them, 'Have you anything here to eat?' They gave him a piece of broiled fish, and he took it and ate in their presence" (Luke 24:39-43).

This physical, glorified body is absolutely essential to understanding the Christian belief of eternal life. Our bodies define who we are, and our personalities and our individuality reside in and arise from our physical bodies. Yes, in many ways we are greater than our bodies; nonetheless, our very existence is predicated on having a body. Such an understanding is most biblical. It is the Hebrew concept of *nephesh*, for which in English translations of the Bible, we employ the term "soul." Life, then, at the moment of death, to use the words from the funeral liturgy, "is changed not ended."

A good way to imagine this process is to consider how we develop here on earth. Our genetic code is implanted at the moment of conception; we grow in the womb of our mothers; we are born and mature into youth, adulthood, and old age. If someone were to look at a photograph of us at three years old, and compare it to a photo of us at fifty, the viewer could have some difficulty in identifying the three-year-old. Nonetheless, we are the same person, and there even could be some characteristics that carry down the years. This process of growth continues after we die. We are the same person, but in every way we increase toward ongoing perfection. This is the promise given to us through Christ's resurrection.

Again, it all comes down to love. Love is never lost. If we continue to live after death, our loved ones will also. The love of parents for their children and children for their parents, husbands and wives for each other, close friends and their mutually deep affections—anyone's love at all is not and never will be lost. And all has been initiated by God first having loved us. Our identities remain after death, but because they are glorified in Christ, the shortcomings, misgivings, regrets, and even sinful behaviors melt away and our relationships undergo constant perfection in ways we cannot even imagine.

Transfiguration/*Theosis*: The Goal of Life

The call of baptized Christians is to become Christ's disciples by following his example throughout our earthly lives. We often hear that doing so will lead us to a positive outcome at the last judgment; specifically, we will gain the rewards of heaven. This concept, however, is only part of the story. If the kingdom of God straddles both the present world and the future one, so too does the Christian life. Eternal life entails a glorified existence in a glorified body, a state that words fail to describe completely, yet since our lives are continuous, we can approximate that glorified state even now.[5] The gospels furnish us with an example of glorification during Jesus' earthly ministry.

In the Christian Tradition, one of the oldest models of glorification in the Christian life can be seen in Christ's transfiguration.[6] This brief passage gives us a glimpse into the glorified state that awaits the ones who pick up their cross and follow Christ. For the disciple, transformation or transfiguration occurs every time he or she engages in an act of charity, love, faith, and hope. We all probably know people whose generosity and compassion toward others in life have so marked them that they are said to glow. For the truly holy person, the glow turns to a dazzling brightness in very many ways, metaphorically and actually. This process is called *theosis*, the act of becoming divine. It is the great exchange promised through Christ's incarnation, passion, death, and resurrection: God becomes human so that humans can become divine, and it starts now even if it will not reach fulfillment until one enters eternal life. But what happens if one falls short of the goal, or misses the goal entirely, or even states from the outset that he or she has no interest in living a life of generous love and chooses the exact opposite? These details will be resolved at the Last Judgment, and angels have a role in this process as well.

Death and Judgment, Particular and Universal

The thought of the last judgment gives many people pause, if it does not cause fear and trembling. Art, music, movies, and imagination show masses of people standing stark naked before the Almighty God. Angels fly to and fro. A portion of the multitudinous crowd is being shoved to Christ's left where heinous, wildly demonic creatures set upon them, stabbing them, eating them, torturing them, and leading them to hell for more of the same forever and ever. The great majority of the mass of humankind, however, are allowed to pass to the right, where angels assist them up into heaven. Every now and then, a demon tries to grab one of the saved, and an angel unfastens the devil's claws. Likewise, some paintings have angels swooping over hell and snatching up a hapless individual who accidentally got into the wrong line. It is a terrifying picture, and one that has caused many to enter the church and many more to leave it.

The Last Judgment is important for any discussion on God, angels, Satan, and demons, for, according to the Christian Tradition, the judgment comes at the nexus of life and death, or the crossing over from one phase of life to another. It is a moment of our greatest insecurity and vulnerability in the face of malevolent spirits. Throughout history, the time when Christians have wanted the angels the most has been at death, for if a demon were going to make a last attempt to snatch a person, it would be at the very moment of death.

Such a view of death, however, runs into conflict and contradiction with the Christian understanding of the Last Judgment and the timing of its occurrence. If we have our final judgment on the day of the resurrection of the dead, when will that be? If it is sometime in the far future, what happens to those who have died before it comes about? Where do they go? In a remarkable paradox, the Christian Tradition makes provisions for both death and judgment at an immediate moment, and for death and a protracted period until the Last Judgment at some unspecified future time. The Roman Catholic liturgical life bears this feature out in its prayers for the dying with a call for angels at the moment of death and the Mass of Christian Burial, which consoles the living by stressing God's loving mercy toward the deceased. This Mass ends with another prayer beseeching the intercession of the angels and the saints.

This explanation of two points within the same expansion of time should call to mind the discussion on the present and future eschatology. Death falls subject to the same principle of the Christian life in which a person lives with a left foot in one time zone and a right foot in another. What follows is an attempt to set out, as clearly as words will allow, the theological foundation for an explanation that presents how Judgment will occur as well as when it will take place. Readers must keep in mind that the descriptions below are based on Catholic theology, experience with the dying, and writings about death and dying.[7]

Personal Judgment: How

Charles Dickens, in his great classic, *A Christmas Carol*, develops Ebenezer Scrooge's slow conversion from a miserly, bitter, cold-hearted boss into a generous, warm, and inviting benefactor by employing in his narrative the Ghost of Christmas Past, the Ghost of Christmas Present, and the Ghost of Christmas Yet to Come all in the span of Christmas Eve.[8] When Scrooge goes to bed, he is one man, and when he awakes the next morning, he is another.

Despite the popularity of *A Christmas Carol*, and running the risk that some might find the story overly sentimental and therefore out of place in a study such as this, it must be said that Dickens nonetheless supplies us with a fine example of the personal judgment. The Ghost of Christmas Past recalls for Scrooge his own pain, sorrows, and disappointments. The Ghost of Christmas Present, by showing him how people view him at the current moment, opens his eyes to how the past is influencing the present. Finally, the Ghost of Christmas Yet to Come lays out for Scrooge a scene of possibilities that he has control over. The harmonization of past, present, and future with the element of free will is the strongest piece in Dickens's novella, and its lessons can help us considerably in formulating the experience of our own judgments.

The "Last Judgment" is a term used that often refers to both the particular, personal judgment and the universal, last judgment. The personal judgment is a review of an individual's life that the individual somehow sees or experiences. Whenever a person has had a close encounter with death, such as a near miss in a car accident, a drowning, and the like, we often hear the situation described with the phrase, "I saw my whole life pass before my eyes." Indeed, studies in near death experiences or in cases when a person has been resuscitated from a point when doctors have considered him or her dead show that the ones who have undergone such an experience will tell how they have reviewed all the good and bad they have done in their lives.[9] Usually, this review spurs the person in question to make the changes necessary in his or her life that will lead to a more positive review when death finally and definitively does come.

One can easily counter that people with near-death experiences are afforded a chance to reform that others are not. There is a strong current in Christian theology, however, which maintains that people always have the choice. Another novelist who describes a wonderful metaphor for this ongoing choice is C. S. Lewis. In *The Great Divorce*,[10] Lewis fashions a plot whereby the souls in hell are given a respite, a vacation weekend as it were, to board a bus bound for heaven.[11] Many make the choice to board the bus, yet some do not.

Lewis describes a good number of characters who ride the bus. One individual relates everything that had happened to him in life and how he finally committed suicide. He lets the protagonist know that while many at the end of the day would take the return journey, which in the story is back to hell, this young man would not. He would stay in heaven where he would find "recognition and appreciation."[12]

There is another section dealing with those who do not board the heaven-bound bus, and a major reason is that they live so far away from the road and, therefore, from the bus stops. At the moment they first arrive at hell, they are so disagreeable and quarrelsome that they have kept moving farther and farther away from their neighbors until the distance to the nearest bus stop is "astronomical distances" away.[13] The most interesting of these far-flung inhabitants is Napoleon Bonaparte, who is described as marching back and forth and never stopping for a moment, all the time muttering, "It was Soult's fault. It was Ney's fault. It was Josephine's fault. It was the fault of the Russians. It was the fault of the English."[14]

Why do so many of the inhabitants of hell refuse to step on the heaven-bound bus? If we use the example of Napoleon (Lewis also mentions Tamburlaine, Genghis Khan, Julius Caesar, and Henry V as residing in the farthest reaches of the place), Napoleon cannot extricate himself from the hell of his own making. Arrogantly belligerent and violent throughout life, he does not change much, if at all, in death. He never sought the mercy of God in life, and he rarely, if ever, showed mercy to anyone else; he does not know how to accept it when offered in death. He and others like him have doomed themselves.[15]

Lewis's *The Great Divorce* is an allegory used to elucidate the Gospel message. For our purposes, a parable in Luke serves as a good example. In the story of the Rich Man and Lazarus

(Luke 16:19-31), we see the rich man who is totally oblivious to destitute Lazarus sitting by his door. The angels are with Lazarus, however, and carry him to the bosom of Abraham, a Jewish interpretation of paradise open to the good and righteous. The rich man remains totally clueless to what righteousness means. In fact, not only does he think that he can still boss Lazarus around, but he also assumes that Abraham is of the same mind (16:24). That he is tormented by flames while Lazarus rests comfortably with Abraham in no way persuades him that he has done something wrong with his life. Abraham's response to the rich man refers to a great, fixed chasm (16:26) that is impossible for anyone to cross. Who fixed it, and why is it impassable?

The rich man himself has fixed it by his failing to heed the law and the prophets and their call for social justice. He has fixed it by treating his material wealth as his right instead of as God's gift. Throughout his life, he placed all his trust in his earthly treasures and never considered the needs of his neighbor. As he lived in life, so he now lives in death. He never crossed the chasm to Lazarus on earth, so he has now sealed his own judgment in the flames of Hades. Is there any hope for this rich man? Yes. In Luke's gospel, a major theme is reliance and trust in God's abiding mercy. All the rich man need do is call out for it, but here is the problem. Since the only reliance and trust he has ever known has been in his own wealth, that now-worthless wealth is all he knows. He cannot call out for mercy. He does not know what mercy is. He never needed mercy from anyone before, and he never showed it to anyone else in life, so he receives what he has measured out.[16] Matthew's treatment of the Last Judgment has a similar theme (25:31-46).

For C. S. Lewis in *The Great Divorce*, all the people in hell who do not choose to board the bus are like the rich man in the parable. Their poor choices in life have precluded their ability to make good choices in death, which brings us back to Dickens's Scrooge. Through the benefit of the three ghosts,

Scrooge can see how his circumstances and choices in life will eventually lead him to a place in his life on earth where he does not want to be, and he changes the way he lives overnight. We can apply the lessons of the gospel parable and *A Christmas Carol* to our Last Judgment.

The Last Judgment is a review of one's life. If we have spent our lives causing suffering or being blind to the suffering of others, if we have never extended a merciful hand to our neighbor, if we have done nothing but foment violence, discord, hatred, and fear among inhabitants of the world, then the hell that we have sown will come back to us. Conversely, if we have been agents of God's peace, if we have comforted the mourning and the sorrowful, if we have thirsted after righteousness, if we have made the lives of others a bit better and a little happier, then the kingdom of God that we have fostered will be ours as well.

All the sinner need do (and we are all sinners, redeemed sinners but sinners nonetheless) is recognize his or her sinfulness and weakness and rely on God's mercy. To be sure, God wills to forgive Adolf Hitler and Josef Stalin and others like them. How likely is it that they would make the attempt to repent and ask for forgiveness? Were they mentally ill? How free from psychological impediments were their choices on earth? Only God knows the human heart, and fortunately, he alone knows how free our decisions are. The worst thing we can do to ourselves is to refuse the love that is offered. The prayers of the angels and saints are working in our favor that we heed the call to repent and enter the fullness of love.[17]

Our Final Cleansing

We have seen that the goal of the Christian life is *theosis*, taking on the divine character that Christ has gained for us through his redemption. We do not always reach our goals in this life, however. What is the final judgment like for the person who, despite all attempts at living a good life, sometimes or even oftentimes falls short of the goal? Is there any way that she can right past wrongs? Well, yes, but not exactly. The review of life or final judgment also entails an active participation on our part. Again, we are talking about a reality that words can never describe adequately. The prayers for the dying and the dead call upon angels and the saints coming to the aid of one at the moment of his death. These prayers also refer to the "perpetual light" and the "light of Christ." At the anointing, the dying person will receive the Eucharist, now called *viaticum* or "bread for the journey" for the occasion. The terminology reflects a forward motion through darkness with something good and glorious at the end.

If we set this movement within the framework of the review of life, we can use an image whereby we walk toward the warm light of Christ as, to use the phrase, "our whole life passes before our eyes." As that life of ours goes past us, we will have a reaction to it, as if we are looking at photos of some past time or event. That reaction will be positive or negative, depending on what we are looking at, just as a photo can remind us of a good or bad experience. Indeed, the case can be made that at the time of this review, the degree of pain we inflict on others will be measured right back on us, as the good we spread will be the good we receive in return.[18]

Hence, this passage through the review can be fraught with dangers. It is not hard to imagine someone freezing at a frame in which he or she did something truly and deeply regrettable. That person can be so overcome with guilt that he may feel that he cannot continue toward the light. Or another person may undergo such sense of shame that she does not see the light for the blameworthiness covering her eyes. Here is where the angels and saints step in. According to Christian belief, as reflected in the funeral liturgies, the communion of saints pray, call, lead, help, and assist that person to the light.[19] Again, Christ does not condemn people to hell, no matter how much evil they have been responsible for in their lives. Rather, we isolate ourselves and, by doing so, condemn ourselves. If a person has refused the light of Christ throughout the totality of her life, what is to say that she will walk toward it in death? Free will continues beyond the grave, and we can still choose or not choose Christ.

Purgatory

Before proceeding any further on this topic, we must clear our minds of anything to do with indulgences, waiting rooms, and temporal punishment. Purgatory is not something the church devises as a means of control, though many have used it that way. Nor does it mean that those who hold to its existence lack faith in the saving power of Christ. We can avoid nearly all these pitfalls if we regard purgatory not as a place but as a process.

Purgatory describes the means by which we choose Christ and let the good we have done mingle with divine grace in order to burn away the dross of our bad choices. We have to want salvation, and for this reason, Dante, in his *Purgatorio*, spurred by the hope of seeing Beatrice, leaps into the refining fire; no sooner do the flames envelop him than he hears a voice beckoning him to paradise (*Purgatorio*, canto 27).[20] Purgatory is the process whereby we confront our shortcomings, our failings, our regrets and let the grace of God burn them away. In this process, in the words of John's gospel, "you will know the truth, and the truth will make you free" (8:32). Facing the truth about ourselves is not always pleasant, but once done, we find that Christ continues to love and welcome us into the realm of increasing love.

In his *Dream of Gerontius*, John Henry Cardinal Newman uses a lake as a metaphor for purgatory (line 901), and, as such, it is a reference to Dante's *Purgatorio*, where in canto 1 the Italian poet calls purgatory the "better waves" as opposed to hell, the "cruel sea."[21] The protagonist, Gerontius (the name is a pun on the Greek, *geron ontos*, literally, "one who is elderly," or "old man"), is lying on his deathbed, and the poem describes his journey through faith, hope, and doubt during the process of dying. Friends and relatives, called "assistants" within the poem, pray along as a priest leads the rites for the dying. By reciting the familiar Catholic litany, they call upon the saints and the angels to lead Gerontius safely to judgment.

Once the soul leaves its earthly body, Gerontius's guardian angel stays with him each step of the way. The doubts and hesitancy that Gerontius had before his death are gone, and there is no terror. Occasionally he hears the voices of those on earth still praying for him. He passes by the loud and bitterly cynical demons who taunt him but who can do nothing more. At the Judgment, the soul "flies to the feet" of Christ and is washed by God's grace. In the last stanza, Gerontius's guardian angel "dips" him in the lake, which the reader knows as purgatory. There is no "sob or a resistance" (line 901). Angels minister to him and prayers from heaven and earth go forth on his behalf until the guardian angel awakens him on the next day, the point where the poem ends (line 911).

Dante and Newman stress that although each person must go through the Last Judgment and purgatory alone, no one does so forlorn and abandoned by God. The angels and saints coupled with the prayers of those on earth are surrounding us every step of the way, and there is a scriptural basis to the works of both of these poets.

In the gospels, particularly Matthew, we have seen how the angels figure prominently in passages dealing with the end of the world and the Last Judgment.[22] They definitely have a role to play in both, and various parts of the Christian Tradition reflect their abiding presence. For instance, a frequent scene in frescoes on church walls and stone carvings above main portals of medieval churches and cathedrals is the end of the world and the Last Judgment; for the Christian imagination, the two events are rightfully combined. In these carvings and depictions, one archangel is most prominent—Saint Michael.

Generally, Saint Michael is portrayed holding a balance. On the archangel's right are the saved; on his left, the damned. Saint Michael weighs the souls and presents them to Christ. The interesting feature is that the souls of the righteous always outweigh the souls of the damned. Satan and his minions see this set of events, and they try to haul down the left dish of the balance. No matter how many demons are involved, and no matter how much effort they muster to swing the balance in favor of hell, the right side with the just and saved is always heavier without a single angel or spirit pulling at it. The angels, in the meantime, are busily escorting the saved into heaven and ensuring that no demon comes anywhere near them.

In the Greek tradition, the interior wall above the central door commonly has a huge fresco of the same theme so that people can view it upon exiting the church. On Saint Michael's left is a large, fiery stream like a lava flow, descending into the even more menacing pit of hell. Yet, this frightening segment occupies barely a quarter of the total space. The other three-quarters are full of the saved ascending *en masse* to heaven, again with angels to help and guide them. In both cases, the lesson is simple: our salvation and not our damnation is the reason Christ suffered, died, and rose, and his mercy always triumphs over our sinfulness.

Last Judgment: When?

If we look carefully at Christian prayers and liturgy, we will conclude that the church has never really decided whether our judgment takes place at the moment of death or at the end of the world. At the same time, the church does not supply a quick explanation on where the dead go as they await the end of the world. The universally accepted assumption is that people die and go either to heaven or hell. Some may allow their imaginations to establish a second round of judgment at the end of the world, but by and large, that scenario is pretty difficult to explain, so no one says much about it. Yet, we profess in the Nicene Creed, week after week, "[Christ] will come again in glory to judge the living and the dead." As with how judgment occurs, I offer the following, which also reflects Catholic theology along with my experience with the dying.

Absolute time does not exist, really. Humans have devised and used time to organize their lives within a chaotic world. The moon and sun have marked the seasons and moments of the day for particular peoples, but they are relative to geography in that spring in the northern hemisphere is fall in the southern half of the globe. Sunrise in Paris is sunset in Honolulu. Scientists even speak of an eternal moment.[23] We can apply the same principles to death.

In the first chapter, we discussed the apocalyptic passages of the Bible. The scenes are pretty dire, with cosmic wars, collapsing mountains, fiery pits, earthquakes, floods, and the like. Truly, anyone who would witness any of these things either singly or collectively would conclude that it is the end of the world. If a person is on her deathbed, struggling for breath, and knowing the end is near, it is perfectly sound to conclude that she is experiencing the end of the world as she has known it. She is filled with doubts about what lies ahead, for it will be unlike anything she has known up until now. If there are any remaining ambitions, they will never be realized, and anything she has built or saved is crashing all around her.

Likewise, people who have experienced terrible news will talk about it as if it were the end of the world. They use phrases like, "Everything came crashing down upon me," and "I felt myself falling into a bottomless pit." They may even physically collapse and fall. At moments such as these, persons at the last stages of dying as well as those who are undergoing a tremendous loss do not really care about some future end of the world, because they themselves are experiencing the end of the world right now.

Simultaneously, we talk about the world we live in and our hopes for children, grandchildren, and all the generations following them; what happens to our descendants is important to us. Those old enough to remember the construction of the Berlin Wall and the Cuban Missile Crisis will recall air-raid drills, nuclear fallout shelters, and detailed instructions on how to survive an atomic bomb blast. Today we see global warming and environmental disaster as the greater threat. The common thread is that these are issues in life that are more communal than personal. Yet, they touch us profoundly.

We can apply many of these details and experiences to the Last Judgment. We live and operate under the artificial construct of time. The moments of our deaths are recorded with day, month, year, and hour. At death, however, time ceases, and one enters into eternity and eternal life. Our particular judgment, according to the manner above, would then take place, for time vanishes. In other words, our individual deaths are our particular judgments. We do not go into a holding pattern until some future date. Indeed, prayers and funeral liturgies reflect such an understanding. These same prayers and liturgies call upon the angels to sustain, protect, and guide us from the final collapse of our earthly lives, through our Last Judgment, and into the *theosis* of eternal life with the communion of saints.

We also profess a final or Last Judgment. In our fears and our imaginations we might consider this final judgment akin to making the second cut for a team, a play, or an orchestra: "I made the first round. Will I also be good enough for the second?" Such a point of view needs a refocusing; it does not accurately reflect a teaching of the Last Judgment that takes into account the limitless love of Christ and his redemption of the world.

Our relationship with God is both personal and communal. God loves us all and has an intimately personal relationship with each of us. As the poet says, however, "No man is an island entire of itself; every man is a piece of the continent, a part of the main."[24] While in our particular judgments, Christ judges the length and span of our personal lives and the degree to which we tried to follow the commandment of love (and it is always the attempt that counts, not the success of the effort), the Last Judgment is how the whole world, both living and dead, throughout all time conducted itself as the communal body of Christ.

Our personal judgment, i.e., the first judgment, occurs through the process of purgatory, as described above. We review our lives sitting under the limitless mercy and love of Christ. The Last Judgment is the communal review, and it incorporates all creation in love. Love is never lost, not between spouses, children, parents, friends, and lovers. Equally, love of creation is never lost either. One of the church's greatest witnesses to this love was Saint Francis and his relationship to the animals, even the wolf. At the communal or Last Judgment, every single person who ever walked the earth will stand together with the angels and saints to witness the culmination of history and creation.

There is no description I can offer about what this communal or Last Judgment will entail or how it will unfold. No one can. When asked about the end of the world, i.e., the end of all universal creation, Christ said, "But about that day and hour no one knows, neither the angels of heaven, nor the Son, but only the Father" (Matt 24:36).[25] Saint Paul expresses best the end of the world and the Last Judgment:

> For the creation waits with eager longing for the revealing
> of the children of God; for the creation was subjected to

futility, not of its own will but by the will of the one who subjected it, in hope that the creation itself will be set free from its bondage to decay and will obtain the freedom of the glory of the children of God. (Rom 8:19-21)

God loves his creation; he does not create the world in order to destroy it, and this love extends to the final moment of the universe. God in Christ is infinitely merciful, and both the first, personal judgment and also the last or communal judgment stand under boundless mercy, and both will be astoundingly glorious for those who choose to be there for each.

Communion of Saints

The communion of saints is comprised of those humans who have undergone *theosis*. The whole celestial hierarchy of angels also plays a part in the communion of saints to the same extent that angels play a part in our earthly lives. It is a common misconception which states that when humans die, they become angels. God creates all angels as spiritual beings who do not have and never have had bodies. God also creates all human beings with earthly bodies who, upon death, will receive glorified bodies.

In the eschatological view of creation, the communion of saints is very present to the living at all times. According to Tradition, the communion of saints prays to God for the living so that those on earth may someday join them. Anyone who has passed through the process of *theosis* is a saint; sainthood is not limited to those who have been declared saints either formally, through the process outlined by the Catholic Church, or informally, by popular acclamation, which had been and still is the case in other Christian churches.[26] This means that relatives, friends, and loved ones are part of the communion of saints, and they are closer to us than most people probably realize.

Within days or hours of the beloved one's death, it is not unusual for people to mention that the deceased husband, wife, mother, father, or child came to them or is present to them. The impression among the living is that those who have passed away are there along with the angels to guide them to heaven. This journey would entail, of course, the Last Judgment, and here the prayers of the saints are particularly important.

In Masses, memorials, or commemorations of the dead, Catholics and other Christians pray for the dead, also called the "faithful departed." In these prayers, Catholics and others also call upon the communion of saints to be present to the dead as well. The aim of these prayers is to surround the deceased with the love of God so that, as they make their way through the Last Judgment, they may see and walk toward the light. If we return to that image of the Last Judgment as a slideshow, the prayers of the loved ones on earth and the saints in heaven encourage the dead to move beyond the guilt and shame into the light of Christ's redemptive love, and the angels assist by illuminating the way.

While the saints are moving the dead toward a life of blessedness, we on earth do not have to wait until we draw our last breath to be close to them. These blessed ones are with us at all times. Maybe we feel their presence; maybe we do not, and whether we do or not is immaterial. They are around without our always being aware of the fact. And with our striving and willing to do the good, and with their intercession, we will one day join them completely and fully in the kingdom of God.

Heaven

Heaven is not a place, despite the fact that in both our secular and religious culture we treat it as such. In the eschatological understanding of creation, it is another dimension of existence; it is the kingdom of God, and that kingdom spans this life as well as the next. We will dwell there in our glorified bodies in the company of all our loved ones and everyone else. The gospels speak of the kingdom as a great banquet, and that image encapsulates this existence the best.[27] It is biblical, and it draws on human experience.

No matter how one remembers great events in his or her life, chances are that a meal and feasting were part of them. Some people may be fortunate enough to recall music, dance, laughter, good food, and good drink. It can also be a holiday meal such as Thanksgiving, Christmas, and Easter that is the occasion for the fond memory. No matter. More than likely, it was such a good time that we may have lost track of the time and found ourselves surprised by the passage of three or four hours. Such a memory or experience is the most tangible foretaste we have of the kingdom of God. All the components are there: warmth; joyful abandon; stimulation of the eyes, ears, and palette. The kingdom is very much like that, according to the gospels and the writings of the saints, but with a difference. The difference between the kingdom at the end of time and now is that, in eternity, it will feature increasing knowledge and joy. Boredom, ennui, and strife will be totally absent. The experience grows in goodness and possibility but is never exhausted, *and* the communion of saints continues the celebration as they help fight the forces of evil who obstruct us on earth. Not a bad deal.

Summary

God created angels as spiritual beings who never had and never will have bodies. They are in service to God and are understood only through their relationship with him. While secular culture and media often refer to angels as independent beings without any reference to God, angels have no meaning or existence independent of him; God creates them as he creates us. Their presence in the heavenly choir and their service to people on earth are a reflection of the divine majesty and glory of the one creator of the universe.

Our information about angels comes mostly from extrabiblical and pseudepigraphic literature, with Gregory the Great and especially Pseudo-Dionysius's seventh-century work, the *Celestial Hierarchy*, forming the organizational pattern and thus the most influential image of angels in the Christian world. With three hierarchies containing three tiers of angels each, the duties of each group, from highest to lowest, is to sing eternal praise to the Lord, to govern the universe, and to deal with human affairs and express the divine love emanating from the Creator toward his creation.

The three archangels, Michael, Gabriel, and Raphael, are the only angels with names that have carried over the centuries, and each is mentioned in the Bible. Inasmuch as guardian angels are representatives of the loving providence of God protecting us from both physical and spiritual danger, they express God's grace. In this sense, they share in Christ's incarnational presence within the church. Just as angels were present to him at various points of his earthly ministry, they are present to us in our sacramental lives.

Christian liturgy echoes the heavenly choir of angels, and in so doing, it maintains the vertical axis of worship—love of God. Crossing that axis is the horizontal outreach of Christian discipleship—love of neighbor. In this sense, angels are integral to the Christian life; as Christians we work to build the kingdom of God on earth, which will find eschatological fulfillment at the end of the world.

People do not become angels at death, yet angels are present at our death as we enter into eternal life, the moment when all parts of our earthly existence reach ongoing perfection. This transformation of the human being into shareholders of the divine life is called *theosis*, a process that coaxes us to let go of sin, guilt, and shame. In the Catholic tradition, this cleansing is called "purgatory." To ensure our passage into glory, the angels focus the light of Christ on us. They escort us along the way as do the saints and loved ones who have gone before us. Our friends and relatives living on earth mix in their hymns and prayers and become part of that glory pulling us through.

Conclusion

Angels are heavenly beings embracing humankind in the love of Christ. They do not act independently of Christ, and, in fact, they have no meaning or existence outside the realm of God. In other words, if we have an experience of an angel, that angel functions in the name of Christ. In addition, that angel performs its service in order to lead us to Christ. Angels exist as part of God's grand plan for the salvation of the universe, a plan that is good, just, and loving. Finally, any angel that claims independence of God, no matter what else it promises, is not an angel but a demon. And so we turn to Part Three.

PART 3

The Diabolical World

As we have seen from Scripture, the kingdom of God begins here and now and is fulfilled in the world to come. In the kingdom here and now, the Christian faith tells us that the Holy Spirit is present among the baptized of Christ's church. Christ's redemptive and salvific act is once and for all time, and nothing can conquer or diminish it. There are forces, however, that since the beginning of time have been trying to convince us to believe otherwise. Welcome to the realm of the malevolent spirits.

In this section, we will discuss the fall of good angels and the rise of bad, the identifying marks of Lucifer, Satan, the devil, hell, unclean spirits, and demons. We will probe haunted houses, devil worship, exorcisms, Wicca, and related fields. We will also investigate the cultural phenomenon of Halloween.

Chapter 8

Satan, the Devil, and Lucifer

The story of Satan's origins has long fascinated people. We have seen in our overview of the Bible that there is really nothing that mentions how Satan came to be. The Old Testament references to him are mainly in Job with most of the biblical citations occurring in the New Testament. The situation is similar for the "devil," with all those references surfacing in the New Testament. "Lucifer," a term meaning "Light Bearer," is the Latin translation of the Hebrew, *Helel ben Shahar* (literally, "Light of the Dawn"), the name of a Canaanite god represented by the planet, Venus, the morning star. Through a short passage in Isaiah (14:11-15), the name becomes associated with Satan before his fall from God's heavenly court. Most likely, the prophet is referring to Nebuchadnezzar, the Babylonian king who conquered Jerusalem. The description of Nebuchadnezzar's pride along with the god *Helel ben Shahar*, or "Light Bearer," inevitably melded this passage into a depiction of a great angel in the heavenly court, named Lucifer, whose unbending arrogance causes him to fall from grace. Lucifer thus becomes synonymous with Satan and the devil.

If there is a paucity of information about Satan's origins within the canonical texts, another body of literature supplies for the lack, the Pseudepigrapha. The vocabulary in the Pseudepigrapha can be confusing, so to clarify: *Satan* is a Hebrew word from Scripture meaning "adversary," someone like a district attorney who would accuse someone of something. The accused would then be obligated to prove his or her innocence. We still operate in this manner when one "plays the devil's advocate" by asking provocative questions in order to test the reliability of another.

Over time *satan*'s meaning gravitated from a legal connotation to one implying an evil being in opposition to God. The word "devil" comes from the Greek *diabolos*, meaning "one who slanders." Eventually, the meaning of Satan merges with the meaning of devil; in fact, in the New Testament, they are synonymous terms. "Lucifer" is a proper name given to the archangel who rebels against God in a body of pseudepigraphic literature called the "Hexamera." Finally, there is the Pseudepigrapha itself. Literally meaning "false writings," the Pseudepigrapha is false in the sense that it is not part of the canonical literature and therefore is not considered by the churches as inspired truth in the same way the biblical canon is.

Pseudepigrapha

The Pseudepigrapha describes a genre of literature that arose during the intertestamental era and that received its inspiration from the biblical canon. The material is speculative and fictional and involves events and persons who appear in the Bible. Most often, the root of the elaborate stories found within the Pseudepigrapha can be found within the canonical Bible, and one such passage supporting the presence of evil beings in the world surfaces in a little-known reference from the book of Genesis.

In the mythological section of Genesis,[1] specifically 6:1-5, we are told that the "sons of God went in to the daughters of humans, who bore children to them" (6:4). This verse has been interpreted among the books of the Pseudepigrapha to mean that angels from heaven married human women. Since this is a boundary that should not have been crossed, the understanding is that evil entered the world in this manner. Moreover, the angels who did such a deed were doing so in an act of rebellion against God. This concept of rebellion also occurs in the literature of the Hexamera, itself an offshoot of the Pseudepigrapha. Of these two versions on the origin of evil beings, the Hexamera becomes the more popular and is, in fact, the basis of the great English epic poem, *Paradise Lost*.

Nearly everything we imagine about the devil's fall from heaven, certainly in the English-speaking world, we know from John Milton's *Paradise Lost*. Besides being one of the great treasures of English literature, at least since the seventeenth century, *Paradise Lost* has inspired most of the imagery for Satan, hell, wicked spirits, and apocryphal battles. Milton's genius, however, lies not in the fact that he wrote the work but rather in how he arranged and used material that had for centuries long been a staple of Christian speculation and folklore.

The hexameral tradition stands as a genre of literature within the much larger genre of the Pseudepigrapha. Scholars trace its origins to the Jewish philosopher Philo (20 BC–AD 50), although shortly after this Jewish philosopher's death, Christian authors further developed it. The basic form of the hexameral works was the "celestial cycle," which describes a rebellion and war in heaven, God's creation of the world, and the fall of humankind.[2] Over the centuries, writers and theologians added to the genre and popularized it: Basil, Gregory Nazianzen, Athanasius of Alexandria, John Chrysostom, Cyril of Jerusalem, Cyril of Alexandria, Gregory of Nyssa, Ambrose, Jerome, Augustine, Hilary of Poitiers, Lactantius, and Marius Victorinus, to name a few.[3] When Milton composed his *Paradise Lost*, he was making a contribution to a literary genre and field of study in which people throughout the ages long had interest.

According to Grant McColley, the hexameral tradition regained popularity in the fifteenth and sixteenth centuries. The invention of the printing press popularized many of the writings of the earlier Greek and Roman theologians, but to these works were added nearly one thousand years of early and late medieval theology.[4] The content of this period concentrates on four themes: (a) Satan's rebellion and the cosmic battle with God, (b) the days of creation, (c) the temptation and fall of Adam and Eve, and (d) biblical history.[5] Milton builds on these hexameral themes.

In summary fashion, *Paradise Lost* begins with the whole hierarchy of angels in a harmonious relationship with God. God then announces his Son will take a place above the angels. No one is disturbed by this presentation until God explains that in the divine plan Christ will become incarnate. At this news, Lucifer, the most beautiful, powerful, and respected among all the archangels, refuses to worship Christ; his pride in his status as a celestial being is wounded by having to adore someone who will take on human nature. To do so is beneath him. Lucifer and his followers depart and rebel. The war they start envelopes the whole cosmic order with a huge battle taking place in heaven.[6] Saint Michael the Archangel defeats Lucifer and casts him and his treacherous army into the lake of fire; from this point, Lucifer's name is Satan.[7]

God commences the six days of creation. On the sixth day, when God creates Adam and Eve, Satan calls a council in hell to devise a way to avenge his disgrace. One way to do so, Satan figures, is to spread chaos within the work God has just created, so Satan enters Paradise and unsuccessfully tries to seduce Eve as she sleeps. Meanwhile, Archangel Raphael visits Adam and warns him of Satan's machinations as he gives the background information for Satan's hatred toward God. Satan enters Paradise again, and this time is successful in tempting the couple into sin. With their fall, sin, death, suffering, and natural disasters enter God's creation. Archangel Michael expels Adam and Eve, and after explaining the major events of the Old Testament to them as a means of showing the consequences of their sin, he promises them a future messiah and savior. He then expels them from Paradise.

It may seem that this short synopsis of *Paradise Lost* summarily dismisses one of the great jewels of English literature. On the contrary, I hope that it will inspire many to read it; it not only is a great epic with masterful use of language but also can supply one with a host of information on the Christian understanding of good and evil over the course of the past two thousand years. John Milton is not the only one who draws from the hexameral tradition to construct his artistry; Dante in his *Inferno* and Boccaccio in his *Decameron* also do so, and everyone should read their works as well.

The importance of these great writers and other authors, artists, musicians, sculptors, and painters of equal merit is that, to this very day, they have supplied us with the symbols, narratives, and characters that have given us a common experience and language to discuss these stories of life, sin, death, and redemption. Their influence has been enduring. Books, movies, videos, and music dealing with evil, the devil, or the occult will often have some references stemming from these classic presentations. Unfortunately, people with little knowledge of the Tradition will employ these symbols as if they were merely props for a show, and for all their efforts they end up with confused facts and little understanding of the whole Christian context.

We can certainly dismiss the hexameral tradition as a series of fabricated and untrue stories, but unless we probe deeper into their content, we will miss a foundational and necessary understanding of good and evil. Certainly, *Paradise Lost* and its forerunners are fantastic in the details, but as always in dealing with truth, it is not always the details that we should be concerned with. The stories in the Bible and even, to an extent, in the

Pseudepigrapha have as their primary focus and objective the truth behind the fact. In every culture and civilization, stories such as those in the Hexamera transmit a truth deeper than the surface narrative offers at first glance. In this case, the reason there is a hexameral tradition is that people have observed and have experienced an evil force which rebels against the good. The how and why of this rebellion constitute the truth beyond the fact, and the hexameral tradition is the human attempt to explain evil using forms, stories, and symbols from the Bible.

Where Does Evil Come From?

The hexameral tradition expresses humankind's greatest fears along with its greatest hopes, but it does not supply an adequate answer to the origins of evil. Inasmuch as the universe is created replete with God's goodness, evil still surfaces. It exists in ways both large and small. Why? What is its origin? Is evil part of God's original plan? If God creates everything, does God create evil? The questions can go on and on, and throughout history, they have. There has never been a completely acceptable response, or at least none that I know of. The best way to answer these questions is to state unequivocally that there is no answer—just as the unfathomable goodness and love of God are a mystery, their opposite, unfathomable hatred and evil, are a mystery. Instead of trying to define from where evil originates or cite its causes, it is better to describe what the sources of evil are not and what is *not* responsible for it.

It is important to recall that we do not inhabit a dualistic universe. Good and evil are not evenly matched, with the forces of good ruling at one occasion and the powers of evil holding sway at another. As we have seen in Christ, the powers of good have overwhelmingly conquered evil; Christ has decisively won both the battle and the war. We have entered the eschatological time through the eternal life his passion, death, and resurrection have gained for us. Unfortunately, some of the stories we have inherited have not always fully reflected this fact, and there are historical reasons for it.

The concept of a dualistic universe is not biblical, not Jewish, and not Christian. Dualism enters the biblical accounts through the earliest Babylonian literature. Later, with the rise of Persia and its religion, Zoroastrianism, dualism exerted a strong pull on Judaism before the birth of Christ. While technically not a polytheistic religion, Zoroastrianism champions one creator, Ahura Mazda, who is the source of all good. Yet, evil has another, independent source, Angra Mainyu, or the destructive principle, which is constantly trying to destroy Ahura Mazda's creation, and the universe is caught in the middle of the strife.[8] At this point, we can see how explaining evil within a Jewish and Christian context can be problematic.

On the surface, it might seem that yes, indeed, there are forces of good and evil in a ceaseless struggle, but to say that these forces are of opposite origin yet equal in strength, power, and authority compromises the whole experience of God as the sole and benevolent Lord of the universe. The theology which developed had to take into account the ongoing human experience of evil; human freedom expressed by free will; absolute sovereignty of the Lord God; and, for the Christian, the fulfillment of God's promise of salvation in Christ. The hexameral tradition, as fantastic as its stories seem, does a good job in balancing these variables. Evil begins at a primordial moment when a sliver of the celestial hierarchy rebels against the goodness of God. Because with free will, these heavenly beings refused to worship the Godhead any longer. They considered themselves equal to God. They battle with the forces of good, i.e., Saint Michael; they are contained for a time until, ultimately, God's own son submits to the worst that evil can deliver and, by doing so, defeats all malevolence.

As we delve into study of the evil forces of the universe, we should keep in mind the essential truths of Christianity, that is, God created and continues to create the universe as an act of love, and what God creates out of love is good; second, Jesus Christ, the Son of the Living God most high, is Lord of the Cosmos and there is no other; third, we humans are destined to become one with God and share in Christ's divinity forever at the fulfillment of the kingdom. Lest it go unsaid, Christians place all their hope and trust in Christ.

Who's Who in Hell

The realm of evil has its own hierarchy of beings, yet, unlike the heavenly court which has its celestial hierarchy amply described by Pseudo-Dionysius, there is not much that is comparable for the rankings in hell. Nonetheless, we can ascertain a status system from what Sacred Scripture mentions. The Pseudepigrapha elaborates the biblical details, and while the information for this source may be pure speculation if not fabrication, the descriptions, names, and means of operating associated with these spirits have become a major feature of folktales and related stories; it is good to clarify references.

When we speak of hell, we do so as if it were a place, and as a place, we consider it a profoundly deep pit in the bowels of the earth. Everything in the culture supports that notion, even grand opera.[9] In Christian theology and belief, however, hell, like heaven, is not a place; rather, it is a state of being. It is absolute separation from God. In conceptualization, we should consider this existence to be the negative and reversed opposite of heaven. So, if God is on top, Satan is on the bottom. If seraphim and cherubim are next in line at the pinnacle of heaven, there are matching evil spirits at the second-last level of hell. Just as in our descriptions holiness increases the closer one gets to God, in hell, evil increases the farther down one goes toward Satan. At the surface of hell, as it were, would be the lesser demons, and at the bottom would be the ultimate, malevolently evil being, Satan. Dante configures his *Inferno* along these lines. To be sure, while this description makes both heaven and hell sound like places, it is a literary device used to enable us to conceptualize the experience of both.[10]

Satan

We have seen how, in the book of Job, Satan begins as an adversary within the heavenly court, something like a district attorney. For all practical purposes, he does not surface again until the New Testament. The term "devil" occurs only in the New Testament, as does "Beelzebul." These three names—Satan, devil, and Beelzebul—refer to one and the same entity; they do not represent three different beings. By the time of the intertestamental period, however, other names were ascribed to Satan.

In chapter 1, we looked at the whole pattern of false worship. The nations and tribes neighboring Israel had their own pantheon of gods whom they worshiped regularly: Molech, Baal, Astarte, Hathor, Amun, Osiris, Isis, Tammuz, and many others. During the Hellenistic and Roman periods, roughly 330 BC to AD 313, gods and goddesses such as Dionysus, Diana, Zeus, Jupiter, Mercury, and Fortuna became part of the mix. The great prohibition that the Lord God placed before the Israelites was not to worship anyone or anything else outside the Lord God. Such a deed was considered apostasy, and if it entailed human sacrifice, as it so often did, the sin of idolatry became even more abominable.

We can observe two simultaneous movements within the biblical narrative and the tradition. One is the multiplicity of other gods, and the other is the move within Judaism from monolatry to monotheism. With the multiplicity of other gods, the question naturally surfaces whether these statues and idols are actually gods at all. We read in the Psalms,

> Not to us, O LORD, not to us, but to your name give glory,
> for the sake of your steadfast love and your faithfulness.
> Why should the nations say, "Where is their God?"
> Our God is in the heavens; he does whatever he pleases.
> Their idols are silver and gold, the work of human hands.
> They have mouths, but do not speak; eyes, but do not see.
> They have ears, but do not hear; noses, but do not smell.
> They have hands, but do not feel; feet, but do not walk;
> they make no sound in their throats. (Ps 115:1-7)

And

> For I know that the LORD is great; our Lord is above all
> gods. Whatever the LORD pleases he does, in heaven and
> on earth, in the seas and all deeps. He it is who makes the
> clouds rise at the end of the earth; he makes lightnings
> for the rain and brings out the wind from his storehouses.
> (Ps 135:5-7)

Recall that many of the psalms reflect a time when the understanding the People of Israel had of their faith was closer to monolatry than to monotheism. On one level, the Israelites see the gods of their neighbors as worthless idols and statues who cannot respond to any human need because they are merely "the work of human hands." On another level, however, the Psalmist says, "our Lord is above all gods," which can be taken to mean that these other gods are living beings but of far lesser stature than the Lord God of Israel. Eventually this qualified view of the Lord God will give way to unqualified monotheism as the people reflect on and learn from their experiences within their covenantal relationship.

When the Israelites faced the false gods on their frontiers and, indeed, when they themselves would run after these idols, it was with the ambiguous view that these gods were, on the one hand, lifeless statues and, on the other, living entities specific to the people worshiping them. In either case, the Israelites were not to have anything to do with these false deities. The biblical record shows that the Israelites' record at obeying the first prohibition in the Ten Commandments was spotty at best, particularly before the Babylonian conquest and exile. After the exile, those Jews who returned to their homeland were chastened in their behavior, and they reinforced their traditional legislation with greater observance. Those who were dispersed went to other places. In some cultures, they were allowed to retain their own practices openly and not forced to adopt the religion of the country they lived in. As Diaspora Jews, they felt sorrow for the loss but also pride in their worship and beliefs.

If we draw conclusions from reading the Pseudepigrapha as well as the literature from the area around the Dead Sea, it seems that the experience in Babylon tipped the balance in acknowledging that the gods of other nations were living beings. Babylon was one of the most magnificent cities of the ancient world. Its ziggurats, made of mud bricks and partially clad in exquisitely enameled tiles, climbed to the sky on a flat, sun-filled landscape. The sight of them must have been spectacular. The Babylonians performed huge religious and secular ceremonies with these structures in mind. Whatever the Babylonians did, it was more magnificent than anything the Jews could remember from their own experience back in Jerusalem. If the Jewish captives credited the Babylonian gods as living beings, it is not difficult to see why. Yet this experience also strengthened the Jews in their monotheism; the writings of Isaiah, Jeremiah, and Ezekiel certainly substantiate that claim. So, the people faced another dilemma. If the Lord God is lord of the universe, over what did these other strange gods rule?

The Jewish experience under the Babylonians lasted approximately sixty years; in 539 BC, Cyrus the Great conquered Babylon and ushered in one of the greatest rules in the ancient world, the Persian Empire. In the history of the Jewish people, one of Cyrus's greatest acts was his liberation of the Jews from their

Babylonian enslavement; they were free to return to Jerusalem and rebuild their temple. After sixty years, however, Babylonian and now Persian influence touched many parts of Jewish life and culture. We have already seen that a dualistic view of the universe is not part of either Christian or Jewish theology; yet the effects of dualism, arising from proximity to such strong and powerful civilizations, made their inroads. For instance, the pseudepigraphic writings display substantial examples of dualistic thought.

Without compromising the singular authority of the Lord God over the whole universe, the people found a way to deal with the polytheistic cults surrounding their Jewish nation. They did so by accentuating the absolute supremacy of God in all things material and spiritual in the universe. The Lord God is the one God living and true. The gods of their neighbors were not true; they were false. It is easy to follow the logic. If these gods are false and counterfeit, they represent a lie. If they represent a lie, they must be liars. If they are liars, they are enemies of truth. If they are enemies of truth, they must be evil. Therefore, these gods are nothing more than the archfiend of the Lord God represented by the names of the devil, Beelzebul, or Satan. As time went on, the names of nearly all the gods in the Fertile Crescent and even the Mediterranean world became associated with the diabolical.[11] A case in point is the synoptic account of the Beelzebul controversy.[12]

It is important to keep in mind that this development of understanding has a legitimate basis in the biblical and theological interpretation. The Holy Spirit works in real time and place. As the faith community grows and encounters new experiences or information, the Holy Spirit finds a way to lead and guide by enlarging, modifying, and shaping theological responses, as the prophets attest. The conclusion that the postexilic Jewish community reached from their experience with the Babylonian gods is that the Lord God and his goodness reign supreme despite the evil manifested in lesser beings. The early church builds on this conclusion and credits Christ for putting the forces of evil to flight. Despite the fact that these evil forces still manifest themselves every now and again, they no longer have and never will attain any stature that can diminish Christ's redemptive act for the universe; the redemption has already occurred.

At this point, a logically thinking person can legitimately ask whether the foreign gods outside the Jewish (and later Christian) frame of reference were really false or whether the Jewish prophets and theologians felt compelled to castigate them thus, so that the people under their gaze and authority would not abandon the Lord God. For if the Jews abandoned the Lord God, the Jewish prophets, priests, and kings would be without a job. In other words, casting the other gods as lying evildoers was part of a way in which the powerful elite maintained their control. Indeed, we can ask this very same question today about the church, the synagogue, and even the mosque: Do the three monotheistic faiths insist on the primacy, sovereignty, and uniqueness of the one, true, living God as a way to downplay and forbid the competition? For Christians, it is a question that returns us to the foundation of our faith.

It would be good to reiterate what we have shown and stated until now. The Christian faith upholds Jesus Christ, the Son of God and Second Person of the Trinity, as the Lord of the universe. Angels and saints are under him and reflect God's love to us human creatures. Satan or the devil, also called Beelzebul, are names of one, former angel who, for reasons of pride and arrogance, refuses to serve God. As a consequence, he has rebelled against infinite goodness and, in so doing, has become infinite evil. Demons are lesser beings who, either as henchmen from the moment Satan turned on God or as former human beings who, in the face of Christ's redemptive love, have chosen to follow Satan. In sum, there are no other gods competing against the Lord God of the universe; there are only evil, lying beings who would like to dupe humans into thinking otherwise. For this reason, at baptism, the candidate is asked (or the parents for the child in the case of infant baptism), "Do you reject Satan, and all his works, and all his empty promises?" At every Easter Vigil, Christians are asked the very same questions again, to remind us that we meet and become one in Christ through the sacraments. In the light of Christ, Satan and his "works" stand out in high relief as manipulative liars.

Summary

The creation of human beings in Genesis inspires the hexameral tradition, that is, stories about rebellion among a certain group of angels in heaven who were absolutely incensed that God would deign to glorify human beings by becoming one of them. This is the great rebellion which John Milton describes in his epic work, *Paradise Lost*. Even before this hexameral tradition mixed with the cults of the great Babylonian and Persian empires, the understanding was that, while other nations might have other gods, the Lord God is the God of Israel and more powerful than the others; this type of theological system is called monolatry. The combination of the hexameral tradition with monolatry produced an understanding in the Jewish and surrounding cultures of a struggle in which good and evil are locked in a battle, and humans must try to ally themselves with the right side.

As time went on, experience, as voiced through the Jewish prophetic tradition, confirmed that there is only one Lord God of the universe who is triumphant over all. Evil is a lesser power when compared to the omnipotence of God. The body of literature called the Pseudepigrapha relates much of this tradition, and it is the tradition that touched so many parts of the culture in which Christ lived. With Christ's ministry, passion, death, and resurrection, all the monstrous fears overflowing from human experience within the world as well as the spiritual and physical paralysis those fears engendered come to an end. The conquest of evil is complete, and we can live in the reality and hope of eternal life.

Chapter 9

Dealing with the Devil

Desert Monasticism

The apocalyptic battles dramatically described in the Pseude-pigrapha should not and cannot be interpreted literally, and no group knew this point better than the monastic women and men, who did so much in shaping Christian theology in the early days of the church. The monks and nuns dwelling in the remote deserts were never far from daily confrontation with demons, as well as appearances of angels, and the stories of their battles with the diabolical world provide us with some of the best thought and practice of living in a world redeemed from sin and death. From this desert literature, we can learn a great deal about how to approach the supernatural in our day.

The monks and nuns moved to the desert to become closer to God. They knew that to abide in God's grace, they would have to battle the demons, who would do everything in their power to keep the holy ones from reaching their goal. The demons were not always external, however; many if not most of them were the internal demons of selfishness, anger, self-centeredness, lust, sloth, envy, and the like. Likewise, expres-sions of grace as seen in faith, hope, and charity are often described as angels and saints in the literature. From our perspective, this might seem to be an application of literary simile in which, say, the vice of anger is depicted as a ferocious demon, but to look at it only as a literary device would not be accurate.

The worldview of the desert monastic men and women was one that drew a very fine line separating the natural from the supernatural realms. Where people today feel uncomfortable with such visual imagery and may even liken it to hallucination, these contemplatives knew quite well how evil desires, forces, and actions could take on a life of their own. A contemporary example that is analogous to such a mindset would be the struggles a person recovering from addictions to alcohol, drugs, sex, and food must face. Moreover, people dealing with personality disorders and mental illness live brave lives with nearly insurmountable difficulties. For them, to fight their way to sobriety or wellness is in very many ways a battle with demons.

The first example involves Saint Evagrius, and the second, Saint Macarius the Great. Before heading to the desert, Evagrius was one of the most learned men in Constantinople. While there, he is overcome with lust for a married, highborn noblewoman, and the woman in question was also smitten with him.[1] At no point in his writings does Evagrius chastise, condemn, or demonize the woman, yet the state in which he finds himself is itself described as falling into the "hands of the demon."[2] Evagrius prays continuously and earnestly for deliverance, and it finally comes in a vision at night of angels dressed as soldiers coming to arrest him. Evagrius thinks it is because the jealous husband had falsely accused him of sexual transgression. In the vision, one of the angel soldiers morphs into the appearance of a very close friend who questions him on the reasons for his arrest.

Evagrius explains all and the visionary friend gives him advice: flee Constantinople. Evagrius, still within a dreamlike state, swears on the gospels that he will do so. He awakens from the vision and realizes that an oath in a dream is still an oath. Immediately, he packs his things and sets sail for Jerusalem, and from there, he goes into the desert.

Did a close friend actually come to Evagrius during the night to speak to him about the impending scandal? Did Evagrius's emotional tension combine with his somnolent state, causing him to see this friend as an angel? Is the whole vision a literary device? For the desert mothers and fathers these questions are uselessly immaterial. The fact of the matter is that Evagrius prayed for deliverance and deliverance came. God loves his people and helps them. A friend is an angel, and an angel is a friend (and we today still use similar language when someone shows up at a time of great need). This story about Evagrius is but one among the desert literature. Within this genre there are many of a more graphic and dramatic nature, as found in an account about Saint Macarius the Great.[3]

A man falls in love with a married woman. She is virtuous and spurns his advances. He in turn becomes so angry that he goes to a magician and pays him to cast a spell so that she would appear as a mare to her husband as well as to all the people in the area. The poor husband is devastated that the woman he loves has turned into a horse; he even tries to feed her hay. No one is able to help the hapless husband restore his wife, so he takes her to Saint Macarius.

Saint Macarius assesses the situation in short order. He tells the husband and those with him that the magician has only made the woman appear to them as a horse; she is still a woman. Macarius further explains that the magician's spell could not possibly change the woman into a mare, because it is not possible for a person to change one of God's creatures into something else. To break the spell, Marcarius sprinkles holy water over the woman's head, and the husband and his friends see the wife and woman they all know. Saint Macarius is not yet finished, however. He also blesses some bread and gives it to the woman to eat with the instructions that she must attend church daily for Eucharist as well as morning and evening prayer. The whole affair had taken place because the woman had been lax in her prayer life and had not been partaking in the Eucharist.

This short passage is a small vignette of the wisdom the desert monks and nuns can offer us today in dealing with the struggle between good and evil. At the very start, Macarius disabuses any notion of dualism; good and evil are not equal, and the forces of evil are subject to God. Although the incident is bad and unfortunate, it is not terror-ridden; God is in control, and there is nothing to fear. Finally, the spell had power only because the woman had not been availing herself of the church's sacramental life.[4]

In many accounts, the demons attack the monks and nuns to the point that the holy ones are left bloodied and bruised. Sometimes the demons tempt the monks with lustful thoughts or may even appear to them as voluptuous women. The demons also pose as guests and try to engage in conversations which would get the monk to renounce Christ deliberately or accidentally.

The desert monks and nuns had other dealings with demons as well. A great deal of the time, the monks exorcised people already possessed by evil spirits. For these holy people, to confront a demon was nothing out of the ordinary. Christ had his temptations and struggles with Satan, and that his followers do as well is all part of the Christian life. As we move into the discussion on the manifestations of evil and demonic possession, it would be good to keep these lessons from the desert front and center, for they form a ready guide on how we should approach the demonic world.

Summary

The literature from the early monks and nuns of the desert recounts some of the battles these holy people had with demons. The followers of the monastic movement went into the desert to become closer to God, and if that meant contesting with demonic forces, so be it. Those battles ensue, for the demons do not want the holiness of the men and women to succeed. One of the greatest contributions that the desert fathers and mothers make is a refocusing of temptation and evil. Rather than directing evil at others, the monks and nuns look first to the evil within; scapegoating is not part of their worldview. Temptation is deception, and the greatest deception is self-deception. Simultaneously, Satan is a very real presence to them, and they do not hesitate to exorcise demons from each other and from people in the neighborhood. The monastic objective was then and is now to follow the light of Christ at all times, and by following that light, monks and nuns lead others there as well.

Chapter 10

The Occult

From the biblical tradition of both Jews and Christians, sorcery, magical spells, and necromancy[1] are very much related to the worship of the polytheistic and pagan cults, and as we have seen, worship of false gods is akin to worship of the prince of all falsehood, Satan or the devil. There is no way to disguise the issue. Participation in the occult is bad and dangerous. It is bad because it enters the paranormal world (i.e., the realm of spiritual entities lying outside empirical explanation) in an attempt to manipulate that world to suit the individual's will. It is dangerous because, once one is in the thrall of malevolent spirits, one has gone beyond the ordinary demonic activity of temptation and has established direct communication with malicious beings.

Spiritual Manipulation

Comparing prayer and worship within the Christian context to the spells and incantations of the occult can help to clarify this discussion. In the Christian tradition, angels and saints are willingly subordinate to the triune God: Father, Son, and Holy Spirit. Their very existence is tied to God's boundless love and mercy and to engendering that same love and mercy wherever they are present. A successful prayer to Saint Anthony for the return of a lost object, for example, occurs only because Saint Anthony is there to show us God's love and will. Saint Anthony does not intervene to draw attention away from God and, consequently, will not grant any petition that itself attempts to promote strife or hatred within another. The end of every petition to Saint Anthony (or Saints Theresa of Liseux, Padre Pio, the Blessed Mother, indeed the whole communion of saints) is our ultimate union with God. Not so the occult.

The occult, as its name implies, is a walk to the dark side. From the Latin word *occultus*, meaning "hidden," the term today most often refers to a *secret*[2] knowledge used to access a spiritual world with harm ultimately coming to all participants. The occult is the general heading under which all sorts of these practices align.

At the very best, the occult is a scam that bilks thousands, and in some cases millions of dollars from overly credulous and unsuspecting persons. At worst, it can ensnare the unaware into the clutches of demonic activity and even full demonic possession. The occult goes by many names, some of which deserve elaboration.

Fortunetelling, seen along beachfronts, in entertainment districts, or in various malls, most often utilizes tarot cards, astrology, palm readings, crystal balls, and such to foretell the future. It is better to exercise caution before dealing with them. Con artists are pros in their work, and they can wrench money from anyone, and the credulous have literally lost their life savings in these establishments. A person of faith should be more discerning; they are the back door into the diabolical world.

Closely related to these trades by virtue of manipulative self-interest are spiritualism or necromancy, Satanism, and the like. The motivation of practitioners is not so much monetary gain—although that also figures into the picture—as much as it is power and control. Furthermore, to everyone's detriment, they are in league with the dark forces of the universe. These practices themselves illustrate why Christian churches condemn them.

Spiritualism and necromancy aim to communicate with the spiritual world, and with the latter, the emphasis is on contacting the dead, but the reason and the goal for doing so are much different from those Christianity holds up. In belief and practice, Christians focus on the Father, Son, and Holy Spirit, around whom are gathered the angels and saints. As explained in chapter 7, the communion of saints bears witness to and reflects the love and glory of God. The angels and saints, while offered devotion for the goodness they bear, are never the object of worship nor do they act as agents independent of the will of God. With Christianity, contact with the dead is superfluous; the living, though it is a different state, share in the communion of saints as do the dead resting in the perpetual light of Christ.

If the whole point is to contact the dead in order to get them to help the living by performing some supernatural act, as it so often is with spiritualism, we must ask how they are offering assistance. If they are not reflecting the redemptive love of God, anything they provide is falsehood. Indeed, the spirit one contacts most likely may not be the person one seeks.

If our loved ones are resting in the divine light of God, they will not make themselves known to anyone on earth through a séance or other conjuring act. To do so would be to put themselves under the power and service of someone lesser than God, under an imposter and fraud. The dead whom we love also love us, and they are not going to put our lives and salvation in jeopardy by following anyone else other than God. No doubt, people will insist that they have met a friend or relative through the efforts of a necromancer, but if the deceased are within the fullness of the kingdom of God, we have to ask who might be the soul manifesting himself or herself to those gathered around the crystal ball and candle. An imposter, that's who.

We must always remember that history as well as the Christian Tradition has shown time and again that the devil and those spiritual beings under him are liars and deceivers. Only evil spirits will allow the living to contact them, and the greatest disguise a spiritual entity can use is to put on the appearance of a loved one. Any time we try to manipulate the spirits, we open the door wide to every sort of infestation, obsession, and even possession. Nothing good comes from Spiritualism or necromancy; serious trouble is always the ultimate result.

Spiritualism

Ouija boards provide a good example of the deception associated with the demonic world. They are derivative of Spiritualism, a movement that arose in upstate New York, particularly around Rochester, in the late 1840s.[3] Purporting to be a system whereby the living could communicate with the dead, Spiritualism became very popular just as the American industrial revolution was taking hold. Its most famous proponents were the Fox sisters who claimed that they could communicate with the deceased. The spirits in turn communicated to the living through a series of rappings whenever the sisters and their guests were gathered around a table for a séance. Despite the fact that the communications were a hoax (the rappings were the result of Maggie and Kate Fox cracking the knuckles of their toes),[4] Spiritualism's popularity did not wane, for other paranormal activity manifested itself in the séances presided over by others, such as table levitation and, through a medium, automatic writing, a phenomenon serving as the precursor to the Ouija board.

A Ouija board may look like an innocent parlor game; in reality, however, it is anything but. The name, "Ouija," is formed by the French and German words for "yes." The alphabet is spelled across the middle of the board with the digits zero through nine written beneath; *Yes* flanks one side and *No* the other. Atop the board is placed a small, felt-bottomed plastic pointer, called a *planchette*. The object is to ask a question as two persons lightly place their fingers on the planchette. The planchette then will slide across to various letters to spell the answer or to respond *yes* or *no* to any question.

To be sure, many of the answers can be attributed to autosuggestion or the psychological state of the individuals involved, but the process does not end there. The supernatural world uses natural means to achieve its ends. The psychological state of a person, especially if that state is in fragile condition, is a ripe receptor for the machinations of an evil spirit, and it always is an evil spirit, because good and blessed spirits work with the will of God; they are not fortunetellers. People who play with Ouija boards end up inviting some bad houseguests into their lives whom they cannot get rid of.

Satanism

Satanism is at the very opposite end of the spectrum from all that is good and holy. It is the complete and unabashed revulsion of God and Christ's incarnation, life, death, and resurrection. In every sense, it is the negative image of Christianity. Satanism has developed its own cultic ceremonies which ape the Christian sacramental system. Often referred to as a "Black Mass," the ritual inverts every part of the Eucharist. For example, prayers are said backward, crosses are upside down, candles are black, and petitions are directed for the destruction of others. In extreme cases, under the notion of a sacrifice, murder may even take place.

It is in Satanism that we see resurfacing the various gods and goddesses of the polytheistic cults that surrounded ancient Israel. The names invoked among the diabolical forces are similar if not identical to the names of the Assyrian, Babylonian, and Canaanite gods: Molech, Baal, Astarte, Pazuzu, Asmodeus, et al.

We can see here how the biblical emphasis on right worship of the Lord God to the absolute exclusion of any other god comes full circle: the gods of the Canaanite, Egyptian, Assyrian, or Babylonian pantheons cannot hold up to the lordship of God. Why? Because God is the Lord of the universe and the other gods are not. If they are not, they lie if they say they are the Lord's equal. If they lie, they are deceivers. If they are deceivers, they lead not to life but to death.

Satanists are not at all reticent in declaring that they repudiate Christ and the salvation he brings. They worship Beelzebul, Satan, or the devil and all the death and destruction lying in his wake. Throughout the scope of centuries, Satanism has always been around. Stories such as Dr. Faustus, novels such as *The Picture of Dorian Gray*, and legends such as Dracula the Vampire all are within the pale of Satanism. In our own time, Anton LaVey founded the Church of Satan based on unmitigated self-centered hedonism.[5] There is absolutely no way Satanism can be reconciled with Christianity. To go with any religious practice that tortures and kills animals and people to satisfy the blood-thirst of some deity is to walk on the dark side, a very dark side.

Summary

The occult turns from the light of Christ and walks in the opposite direction. It engages in spiritual manipulation for personal gain. Incantations, séances, Ouija boards, tarot cards, fortunetelling, mediums, psychic arts, and all such practices are dangerous. They can lead a person into spiritually and physically damaging situations. Most cases of demonic possession begin with practicing the occult.

Spiritualism and necromancy are closely aligned with the occult. They are not ways to contact deceased loved ones. Contact with our loved ones is made through prayer and by partaking in the sacraments. Beloved family members are within the communion of saints, and that same communion is looking out for us. To engage in spiritualism and necromancy is a shadow away from practicing the occult.

Satanism is the complete and utter rejection of God. Satanists worship Satan in all his guises: Beelzebul, Lucifer, Asmodeus, and Molech. Satanism is hatred of all that is good and holy, including all creation and all God's creatures.

Chapter 11

Satan's Activities

> See to it that no one takes you captive through philosophy
> and empty deceit, according to human tradition, according
> to the elemental spirits of the universe, and not according to
> Christ. (Col 2:8)

For most, information on the occult, demonic possession, haunts, and the like comes by way of folklore and Hollywood, and both concentrate on the spectacular and sensational. In actual fact, Satan's world is the world of sin, and sin can be very banal. It is not too much of an exaggeration to say that sin thrives on neglect—neglect of self, of loved ones, of neighbor, and of the suffering of the world. Indeed, Satan's greatest victory is to have humankind think that he himself and sin do not even exist. One has to wonder whether the recent increase in possession and exorcisms might not be part of the devil's plan to keep our attention away from his far greater presence in the world of environmental destruction, rampant consumerism, violence, and wars of all kinds. Discussion on temptation, infestation, obsession, oppression, and possession cannot take place outside the context of Christ's redemption.[1] To do so is to live an illusion and grant Satan too much power, and that is exactly what he would want to hinder creation's ultimate union in Christ.

Temptation

By far the most prevalent form of evil in the world throughout history is temptation, and temptation is the result of free will. We cannot choose to do good if there is no other option, and if there is no other option, we are not free agents, and if we are not free agents, our existence is not the result of God's love. Without free will, we would be mere automatons in some cruel, supernatural joke. A temptation is the urge or impulse to commit a wrongful act or to omit performing a good one. Temptations can be small, such as lying about one's age to get a discount, or large, such as embezzling thousands of dollars from a place of employment.

There is nothing dramatic about temptations, but the evil and suffering caused by lies, injustices, sarcasm, and adultery make successes in temptation the devil's greatest victories. In the teaching and experience of the desert monks and nuns, the best way to overcome temptation is to desire to live a holy life and to pray to God for the strength and ability to do so. For the Christian, partaking in the sacramental life of the church is the greatest aid for combatting temptation.

Infestation

When certain locations, buildings, or objects are subject to unexplainable phenomena, particularly repulsive activity or presences, the place is said to be "infested," or, more colloquially, "haunted." The term "haunted," however, may not necessarily imply the presence of a demon; the stories behind many haunted houses seem to indicate that the mischievous spirit may be some person who has died and is not able to let go of this world.

For instance, the resort town of Cape May, New Jersey, presents itself as one of the most haunted cities in America, and the stories behind such houses, with some notable exceptions, have a common theme of unfinished business or a tremendous burden of guilt: A mother who forgot to lock the nursery door of her house discovered her child had crawled out to the trolley track and was run over. The ghost of the mother walks the halls to this day, locking all the doors. In a hotel, a maid fell to her death trying to sneak out to meet her boyfriend. Guests report the sound of heavy objects being dragged across the floor, doors opening and closing by themselves, etc. Some have also reported seeing the ghost of the young woman peering out the upstairs window.

Similarly, members of a religious order conducting a Catholic high school in New England were awakened one night by loud banging on all the walls leading down a long hallway. The lights flicked on mysteriously as they illuminated the corridor to the school's classroom and ended there. The people in the building connected this activity to a teacher who had died in that classroom several years earlier. To remedy the problem, the school chaplain said a Mass in the same room for the repose of the teacher's soul, and all such haunting activity ceased.

The stories from Cape May and New England characterize a type of infestation that is nonmalicious and actually fits very well into the Roman Catholic funeral ritual, in which the faithful pray for the repose of a person's soul within the perpetual light of Christ. The teacher, it seems, needed some more prayers in order to follow the divine light. In many cases similar to these, tremendous guilt within the person at the time of his or her death is often the chain that tethers her to a particular spot. The blessings and Mass make the love and forgiveness of Christ known to her. In New England, it appears that the infestation met a blessed end. It is unknown about the mother and the maid in Cape May. Unfortunately, the operators of many of the inns and hotels there do not allow any kind of Christian exorcism that might help the ghost move on; guests come to experience the presence of a ghost, and the owners do not want to let them down.

While the above examples give every indication of being a benign cry for help, there is a kind of infestation that truly indicates evil activity and demonic presence. Sites of human or even animal sacrifice, spiritual manipulation, prostitution, murder, and suicide are all prone to infestation. A cursed object implanted within the premises can also bring about demonic activity. As with the benign type, exorcists deal with malicious infestations by blessing the locale or celebrating a Mass at the place.[2]

Oppression

The gospels relate cases of oppression (Matt 17:14-18; Mark 9:21-25; Luke 13:10-16). Moreover, the monks and the nuns of the desert have written about being physically attacked by demons, and witnesses would see their bruises and welts. Exegetes have attributed two of the above biblical accounts of oppression to known medical conditions such as epilepsy (Matt 17:15 says as much) and curvature of the spine (Luke 13:11).

It is most important not to attribute a personal sin as the cause or reason for a person's suffering any ailment or infirmity—physical, psychological, or mental. In other words, God does not punish anyone for sinning by smiting him or her with sickness or disability. Christ is explicit about that point in Luke 13:1-13. When Christ cures the woman, he is pointing to the fullness of our eschatological lives when all things will be well.

Demonic oppression, on the other hand, leans more toward a physical attack.

> The Enemy, however, could not stand his being there. He was afraid that little by little Antony would turn the desert into a city of asceticism. Coming out one night with a mob of demons, he beat Antony with so many blows that

he was left lying on the ground, unable to speak because of the torturous blows. Antony said with certainty that human beings could never wield such blows or inflict such punishment, so great was his suffering.

But by the providence of God (for the Lord does not disregard those who hope in him), the next day Antony's friend came, bringing some bread for him. (*Life of Saint Antony* 8)[3]

The holiness of Saint Antony of the desert prompts the devil to attack him in an effort to intimidate and discourage him, and this is not the first time Satan does so. Saint Athanasius's *Life of Saint Antony* is replete with stories of physical conflict with demons. Initially, the demonic raids take the form of temptations, but having no success with the saint, the evil forces keep upping the stakes. In the example above, Saint Antony willingly stays in the tombs overnight for the express purpose of battling the devil's forces and to prove to the tempter that he, Antony, will not be intimidated. Generally, Satan oppresses the most holy in order to force them to despondency and thus lead astray all those who take inspiration and solace from them.

Obsession

Demonic obsession has nothing in common with obsessive compulsive disorder (OCD). OCD is a medical condition manifested by certain intensely repetitive actions, such as hand-washing, and can be controlled and greatly diminished through therapy.

Rather, a person afflicted with demonic obsession will feel fixated on a particular idea or plan of action which usually involves harm to oneself or others. Depression and overwhelming sadness usually accompany demonic obsession. Prayer, participation in the sacraments, and spiritual direction can bring one some relief. Yet, demonic obsession is as difficult to explain as it is to diagnose. Demonic obsession is a repetitive evil or revolting thought that will not leave the mind. These symptoms, however, also describe certain psychological conditions.

People with borderline personality disorder (BPD) can become extremely fixated on ideas and actions that will harm themselves or others. Many would describe these fixations as evil and disgusting. Unfortunately, people with BPD are often very depressed and sad, almost beyond the ability of drugs to treat successfully. Yet this condition is in the psychiatric diagnosis manuals, and it is not described as demonic obsession. Good and qualified spiritual directors will not even approach people with BPD until the person has undergone successful medical and psychological treatment. In fact, spiritual directors are trained to be able to tell when a severe, untreated psychological condition is manifesting so they can suggest the person seek psychological treatment. One spiritual director writes, "I know when evil is manifesting—and when a psychological condition is not the issue. . . . The main manifestation is extreme resistance and challenge to God, prayer, and Scripture. It can also surface as a personal attack on the spiritual director. It is frightening; good spiritual directors use sacramentals to protect themselves and others. I myself carry a blessed medal of St. Benedict or St. Michael as well as a relic of St. Padre Pio."[4]

Possession

The most discussed, feared, and yet dismissed among all the works of Satan, demonic possession is rare, but it does exist. The subject of novels, movies, and documentaries, possession grabs the attention of believers and nonbelievers alike. Most people receive their information about demonic possession through movies or cable television networks. Unfortunately, these media aim to attract large audiences and so are geared toward sensationalism. Accuracy and truth suffer in the process. We should be careful about the information pulled from the internet, because groups, even well-meaning Christian groups, can be overly zealous to see demonic possession in people who are dealing, or should be dealing, with other issues.

The great share of the biblical witness for possession is found in the gospels. Christ comes to the world to redeem it. This creation belongs to God, and physical, spiritual, and material wholeness are part of the promise of redemption:

> When he came to Nazareth, where he had been brought up, he went to the synagogue on the sabbath day, as was his custom. He stood up to read, and the scroll of the prophet Isaiah was given to him. He unrolled the scroll and found the place where it was written: "The Spirit of the Lord is upon me, because he has anointed me to bring good news to the poor. He has sent me to proclaim release to the captives and recovery of sight to the blind, to let the oppressed go free, to proclaim the year of the Lord's favor." (Luke 4:16-19)

The captivity and oppression mentioned in Luke's account are both physical and spiritual. The unclean spirits and demons whom Jesus encounters know this and even proclaim him as Lord. To be sure, many of the diseases and ailments described in the Bible are medical conditions that were unknown as such in antiquity. At that time, there were not the drugs or medicines we have today to curb and alleviate many of the symptoms of mental and emotional illness; what passes for possession in the gospels can easily be confused with psychosis or severe depression.

Yet, illness does not explain it all, and, in fact, many of the stories differentiate between physical suffering and the oppression caused by an unclean spirit,[5] a demon,[6] and Satan.[7] Our modern answers do not answer everything. The church continues Jesus' earthly mission and makes Christ present in the world. What people suffered in Jesus' day, people suffer now. What

Jesus encountered in his ministry, the church encounters in its ministry today. We should not, therefore, consider demonic possession and its cure, exorcism, as anachronistic.

The church has always engaged in the ministry of exorcism. We not only see Christ casting out demons in the gospels but also read of Paul doing the same thing (Acts 16:16-18). The early monks and nuns of the desert were well acquainted with exorcisms, and saints have continued the practice up to today. The Roman Catholic Church, however, has never been casual in performing exorcisms; it has a tight set of criteria to determine demonic possession that have been clarified and adapted throughout the centuries. In fact, the last time the policies for exorcisms were updated occurred as recently as 1998 under Pope John Paul II.

Signs of Possession[8]

As we have seen from some of the biblical accounts, what at an earlier time may have been considered signs of possession, at a later point in history would be seen as a physical, mental, or emotional illness. For this reason, the church proceeds very cautiously before determining whether a particular person is suffering from demonic possession. There is not a gradual progression among the attributes listed here. For possession, they cannot appear singly but rather frequently in any combination and in any order. The exorcist must be morally certain that these signs do not have any medical, psychological, or parapsychological explanations:

- ability to speak and understand foreign languages well beyond the level of any education one may have received or outside the opportunity to have heard

- knowledge of information beyond what the victim can know, such as past unconfessed sins of another individual and secret, confidential information of others

- ability to predict future events

- intense and unbridled hatred for holy things, such as relics, holy water, sacramentals, and pronunciation of the sacred names of Jesus Christ, Lord God, and the Blessed Virgin Mary

- evidence of strength well beyond a person's age, physical condition, and normal human ability

Although different Christian denominations have their own methods for performing exorcisms, within the Roman Catholic Church, the bishop is the one who makes the determination that a case should go to an exorcist. The exorcist must be a priest appointed as such by his bishop, though a bishop himself can also be an exorcist. To qualify for this office, an exorcist must be holy, prayerful, of sound devotion toward God as exemplified by a life of prayer and study. He must also be experienced in discerning spirits and in reading souls.

The exorcist should approach cautiously a request for exorcism, taking into consideration the signs of diabolical possession. He must thoroughly test any doubts he may have on whether there are other explanations for the phenomena he is seeing. Ideally, there should be a team of priests, doctors, and psychiatrists who make the initial investigation. If all evidence points to full demonic possession, then the exorcist goes to the next step.

The exorcist must prepare for his duties with prayer as well as fasting, heeding Mark 9:28-29. He also receives the sacrament of reconciliation before undertaking the exorcism, since the devil, as the Prince of Lies, will often try to intimidate an exorcist by relating his whole biography and struggles to all within earshot. He will also mix lies with twisted truths. The sins one has confessed, however, are off limits, for Satan has no access to them and cannot know them. The exorcist will gather with the family and friends of the possessed individual to ascertain when the signs of possession first became apparent. The victim may have been the subject of a curse, so the exorcist should check that detail. He will enquire if the possessed or any family, friends, or acquaintances have been involved in spiritualism, séances, tarot card and palm reading, fortunetelling, and Wiccan rituals. If so, all parties must agree to cease that activity immediately and never return to it. Finally, he has to ask the victim whether he or she wants the exorcism. If the possessed person does not, the exorcist goes no further with the ritual; free will is always central, even in demonic possession.[9]

Ideally, the exorcism should take place in a church, where the presence of so many blessed objects sanctified by so much prayer will work to the demons' disadvantage. In fact, the possessed, when in a period of lucidity, will often seek out a church or holy place on their own. Unfortunately, performing the exorcism in church is not always possible, in which case the exorcism takes place at home.

The exorcist takes with him a crucifix, which should always be visible during the ritual, holy water, and the relics of a saint, particularly one known to have combated evil spirits, such as Padre Pio. At various points, he will apply each directly on the possessed, for demons cannot stand to be around anything holy. In fact, if it becomes evident that certain saints' names, relics, or holy objects cause greater pain for the demon than others, these should be used with greater frequency.

The ritual warns the exorcist not to converse with the unclean spirits. To do so is to grant them too much dignity, but also makes one susceptible to the spirits' lies. Even if the demon insists that he is a good spirit, he must not listen to him. The Prince of Lies and his ilk are all skillful and masterful liars.

Nonetheless, there is a regular set of questions the exorcist is instructed to ask the demons: (1) the name and the number of the demons possessing the individual (Mark 5:9; Luke 8:30),

(2) when and where they took possession of the person, and (3) why they entered the person. The exorcist then orders the demons, in the name of Jesus Christ, to depart. This ritual is repeated until the demons are gone, and sometimes it takes years.

Causes of Possession

> When the unclean spirit has gone out of a person, it wanders through waterless regions looking for a resting place, but not finding any, it says, "I will return to my house from which I came." When it comes, it finds it swept and put in order. Then it goes and brings seven other spirits more evil than itself, and they enter and live there; and the last state of that person is worse than the first. (Luke 11:24-26)

Outside of those who are truly engrossed by and bound to evil, the reason for all the interest in demonic possession over the years is based on our own fears; most people are petrified of being possessed. The media, especially the entertainment industry, add to the interest by portraying possession in its full, graphic reality. This situation is sad and unfortunate, for Christ has come into the world to rid us of such fears. Christians must never forget that Christ is Lord of the universe, and Satan along with his minions is subject to him. While saints have been oppressed by Satan, none has been possessed by him. This detail furnishes us with insight into the causes of possession: absence of the good and holy attracts the evil and accursed.

Before undertaking the ritual of exorcism, the exorcist does all he can to ascertain the background and history of the one possessed. Generally, he will discover something that has occurred to invite the demons in. Even in the industrialized world, participation in the occult more often than not has provided demons the gold-plated invitation to take up residence in a person, and for this reason, the church throughout history has condemned fortunetelling, necromancy, and Spiritualism in all its guises and forms. In other cultures, especially in mission countries, a person who is possessed frequently has been the object of another's curse. Nonetheless, there are a sufficient number of cases of possession among the most modern and technologically advanced countries that have also been caused by a curse.[10]

As noted above, the exorcist must seek the permission of the possessed person in order to execute the exorcism; some possessed people have declined the offer. As incredible as it may seem to one striving in the Christian life, there are people who prefer the vain promises of the devil—for example, the subject of the famous legend of Dr. Faustus.[11] It is to our benefit to keep in mind that Satan hates God and therefore hates everything God has created, primarily us. If a deal looks too good to be true, it is; the devil is the chief of all lies and falsehood, who spends his time getting us to believe his empty promises.

The demons themselves have given us other reasons for why they take up residence in an individual. In the story of the Gerasene demoniac, we read, "They begged him not to order them to go back into the abyss" (Luke 8:31). Exorcists often find the demons making similar comments.[12] Perhaps the demons wish to continue their mischief making, which they cannot do from hell. It is also logical to conclude that hell is such a cursed and awful place that not even its own spirits want to dwell there, and this stands to reason. Hatred is all encompassing, and its intensity in the bowels of hell makes it unbearable for its own inhabitants. Our imagination fails to grasp it. It also explains why the exorcist seeks to discover whether the possessed is suffering from any deep-seated anger or inability to forgive; rage, hurt, and spite, even if we are suffering a gross injustice, are the seedbed of diabolical machinations and a good home to many demons.

A house "swept and put in order" can also be empty, which is the point of the parable above. Demons move into a person because there is nothing there to keep them out. For those who strive to follow the gospel, to forgive others their offenses, to frequent the sacraments, to engage in acts of charity, to work for social justice, to promote peace—in sum, to love God and neighbor—there is absolutely no reason to fear Satanic or demonic possession.

Summary

Satan's activity in the world is divided into temptation, infestation, oppression, obsession, and possession. Of the five types of activity, possession attracts most of people's fear and attention. There are set criteria the church uses to determine demonic possession as well as choosing priests to be exorcists. The cause of demonic possession is usually participation in the occult, though being placed under a curse by someone is not infrequent, especially in mission countries. A person who lives close to prayer and the sacraments need not fear demonic possession.

Chapter 12

Neo-paganism

The discussion on monolatry, monotheism, and dualism opens larger questions on religious pluralism. Obviously, not everyone in our towns and neighborhoods, let alone the whole world, is Catholic or Christian. If Christians are going to make the truth claim that there is one God in the universe (a claim that both Judaism and Islam also make),[1] how does a Christian operate in a world where a good many people worship other deities within other faith systems?

Living in a pluralistic culture as we do, where freedom of religion is a guaranteed human right, which no one can impinge upon or hinder, we must, as good citizens, recognize the right of individuals to choose to worship whom and how they wish. Since we hold this freedom as a basic human right guaranteed universally in nearly all democratic societies, we cannot and should not do anything that would restrict it. Such is the understanding on a civic and political level that allows our society to live in peace and justice.

On the theological or even philosophical level, a different dynamic enters the discussion on faith and belief. Many make the mistake of using this necessary and fundamental civic and political right to determine the truth claims of every faith. Upholding freedom of religion for the good of society does not mean that all religions are alike in what they profess. The Catholic Church rejoices in truth wherever it may be found. For example, Christians have much to learn from Buddhists and Hindus when it comes to peace and nonviolence. Theologically, the church sees Christ in all goodness and truth even if adherents of other faith systems do not. Nevertheless, the discussion on the claims of other religions takes a different turn if another religion, Satanism for example, does not have the true, good, and beautiful as its aim.

Neo-paganism and other forms of New Age are polytheistic by nature and take as their point of departure a rejection of the monotheism advanced by Christianity particularly, but also by Judaism and Islam. Depending on the individual, this rejection can range from apathy to outright hostility. Unlike Hinduism, Buddhism, Taoism, or even the animist belief systems of tribal cultures, New Age and Wicca are products of Western Civilization, despite the fact that many of their adherents claim they arise from older, ancient cults, whether those cults be in the Americas, Europe, Mesopotamia, India, China, Egypt, or Polynesia. In other words, New Age and Wicca are a reaction to Christianity, particularly Western Christianity, which is why these movements are referred to as "neo-paganism" by their adherents. Whereas the theological and lived expression of Christianity is communal and relational, the varied belief systems and visible forms of New Age and Wicca are individualistic. There is no dogma or prescribed way of life, and for this reason they often have an affinity to another Western phenomenon, secular humanism.

New Age

There is not much to say about New Age that has not been said before, long before. We can certainly look to the Theosophical Movement[2] that had its origin among a certain group of intellectuals in late nineteenth-century Europe and North America, but in actuality, we can go back much further than that to first- and second-century Gnosticism.

Gnosticism is a syncretic system of thought encompassing nearly every major Mediterranean philosophy and religion of the intertestamental era. Judaism, Christianity, Stoicism, local gods, and imperial cults all have influenced Gnosticism with the result that it is nearly impossible to explain or define it conclusively. There are two salient characteristics of Gnosticism, at least in how they pertain to Christianity: (1) the openness of salvation only to those who properly understand the mysteries or secret knowledge that its adherents profess and (2) the disregard for the human body and all created matter.

Without any creed or set of teachings, people of that time interpreted Gnostic thought however they saw fit. Such a belief system was attractive to many, especially the rich, the wellborn, the well-educated, and men. The thought system, however, never really vanished. It has run through the centuries up to the present time and has found a home in New Age.

In a word, New Age is Gnosticm in contemporary idiom, and for various reasons, it has many followers today. All too often, one can argue, dogma and orthodoxy appear to be too turgid and dense to be taken seriously. Worshiping according to a particular faith and tradition also takes commitment and makes demands, and in a society that stresses individual freedom, life built on communal obligations and celebrations is too constraining.

As good as individualism can sometimes be, it can also be found wanting by its attendant loneliness and disconnection with community. It is also possible that those who adhere to New Age do so because the rank individualism of society is absent of divine love and sacred mystery. The attraction to crystals, the great Ground of Being, astrology, and the like reflect this lack, and people try to fill the void with amulets and esoterica. And there is the far bigger issue of salvation.

In Christianity, salvation is through the passion, death, and resurrection of Christ and is open to all. There is a path to follow and the Son of God shows us the way. In early Gnosticism, salvation was restricted to the fortunate few, and it never included the body or eternal life. In its lineal descendent, New Age, how and to whom salvation is meted out is not much different. The spirits and angels that often make their appearance in New Age culture are not connected to Christ or his sacraments. As we have seen in our discussion thus far, spiritual beings unattached to God are very dangerous.

Wicca

Wicca as a movement dates from the late nineteenth century. It sees itself recapturing the folk religion of northern Europe before the arrival of Christianity. Many of its claims, including the insistence that it dates from before AD 500 and has gone along unchanged since that time, have been proven false.[3] Nonetheless, Wicca, as it exists today, has its own practices and belief system, which demands a discussion of whether or not there is a historical root to it.

Etymologically, the Anglo-Saxon term *wicca* gives us the contemporary English noun "witch," a word loaded with connotations of curses, spells, and devil worship. The topic of witchcraft is a very sensitive one today owing to the fact that in history, especially after the Reformation, many women but also men were executed by various princes, kings, and governments. In most cases, these actions were performed with the reluctant participation of the churches, because the evidence of guilt for being a witch was founded on the most circumstantial of evidence. Not even were the American colonies spared; Salem, Massachusetts, had its infamous witch trials in 1692, proceedings that had more to do with petty spites and property claims than collusion with the devil, yet devil worship was the accusation, and innocent people were put to death.[4]

When people speak of Wicca today, however, they are referring to a different entity altogether. Proponents of Wicca maintain that their religion is what existed in northern Europe before
the arrival of Christianity, when fertility cults closely tied to the
sun, moon, and change of seasons were the system by which
people ran and understood their lives.[5] Wiccans claim Christianity
destroyed this religion and persecuted its followers; persecution
resurfaced, they assert, when those people who maintained the
old religion found themselves the object of attack in the early
Modern period; Wicca today is a return to the pre-Christian
religion.[6] In actual fact, Wicca is an outgrowth of nineteenth-
century romanticism that became popular in the 1920s and
1930s.[7]

Regardless of the debate on the origins of Wicca, the fact is
that Wicca exists now and has its adherents. Primarily worshipers
of nature, and as polytheists and pantheists, Wiccans refer to
the goddess(es) and the god(s). Wiccans do not believe in the
Lord God of the Bible and in many ways are quite hostile to
monotheism, seeing it as patriarchy at its most oppressive, an
unfortunate and inaccurate position. Nowhere does the Lord
God refer to Godself as male. In the appearance to Moses in
the burning bush, the name given for the deity is, "I am who
I am" (Exod 3:14). Moreover, the prohibition against fashion-
ing any images prevents exclusive gender specification (Exod
20:4). This statement does not deny that the biblical writers
and subsequent translators have assumed that God is male, but
in reality, God is neither male, female, neuter, or hermaphro-
ditic. God is God and goes beyond the human limitations of
language and comprehension.

Magick

Spelled with a final *k* to differentiate it from circus shows,
magick refers to the practice of manipulating the spiritual world
in order to accomplish one's will. Wicca makes the distinction

between *black magick* and *white magick*. Black magick is seen as that which colludes with the demonic world to bring down curses, spells, and harm upon another, while white magick deals with good spirits and seeks only to help oneself without harming another. Followers of Wicca insist that they engage in white and not black magick, maintaining that since they do not believe in the Christian God, they do not believe in Satan, either. Those who practice magick, either white or black magick, hold that it is their form of prayer. Christians pray to be in contact with their God; Wiccans use magick to be in contact with theirs. Magick and prayer are far from the same, however.

Magick and Prayer: The Difference

The differences between prayer and magick are best explained through example. Let's take the problem of financial stress. If a person has lost a job and is facing severe financial hardship, within the context of the Christian life, he or she will pray to God for help and strength to carry on. The aim is not to alter God's will. Rather, the aim of our prayer is to strengthen our trust and faith in God knowing that God never abandons us despite the strain we might be undergoing. Trusting in God allows us the freedom to be open to his abundant grace and to avail ourselves of the opportunities he might send our way. With God, we can carry on and overcome the hardships of this world. This approach is a much different mindset from practicing magick to accomplish one's ends.

A person resorting to black magick would deal with this same problem of financial hardship not by faith and grace but by manipulation, deceit, and violence through perhaps casting a spell that would bring harm to one's creditor, or through using malevolent spirits to assist in embezzling funds, or through enacting violence on another to steal the fortunes left in his or her will. In black magick, there is no trust in divine Providence because there is no belief in the love of God. The spiritual forces into which one places his or her trust are even more selfish, hateful, and cruel than we can make ourselves out to be.

Applying the same problem of financial stress to the practice of white magick, a person could employ spiritual beings to ensure that he or she wins the lottery. Is anyone harmed? The ethics and morality of state lotteries and the way they take advantage of those who have the least is well beyond the scope of this study; suffice to say, if there are winners and losers, a Christian has to be concerned about the losers. Focusing on spiritual manipulation to win the lottery obviously means that some kind of machination will take place to guarantee that the one who went to the sorcerer will win, even if it means that the person who really had the lucky ticket finds out that it is lost, while the one who did not suddenly finds that same ticket in his or her wallet. Here, too, there is no trust in divine Providence and no belief in divine love. The spiritual forces one uses are a projection of one's own avarice, and because they are, many questions arise regarding the difference between white and black magick.

White and Black Magick: Is There a Difference?

Those who practice white magick may claim that they have good intentions at heart, and they may sincerely insist that they are in contact with only good spirits and not malevolent ones, but the line between a good spirit and a bad one is really nonexistent. Spirits summoned under the guise of white magick may, at first, seem to be good, friendly, and helpful. It is to be expected that they are. No one is tempted by a revolting personality; Satan, like a con artist, may be evil but he is not stupid. As the example of the three different ways to solve financial difficulty show, the difference between white and black magick is not in kind but only in degree. Both have the self at the center of discussion. Hence, it is the age-old story of worshiping the creature instead of the creator.

The biblical and lived tradition of Christianity, however, has shown us that once we shift the focus from the Creator of the universe to the creation itself, which in the biblical tradition is the essence of idolatry, we open ourselves wide to the Prince of Lies. An evil spirit can manipulate the truth and deceive us very well. How do we know that the good and friendly spirit we invoke is not a malicious demon in disguise? Initially, it may be difficult; ultimately, there will be no mistaking the two. Followers of Wicca may be earnest and sincere in their desire to consult only good spirits, and the evil spirits take full advantage of their naiveté.

Christianity and Neo-paganism

> Long ago God spoke to our ancestors in many and various ways by the prophets, but in these last days he has spoken to us by a Son, whom he appointed heir of all things, through whom he also created the worlds. He is the reflection of God's glory and the exact imprint of God's very being, and he sustains all things by his powerful word. When he had made purification for sins, he sat down at the right hand of the Majesty on high. (Heb 1:1-3)

Christianity's encounter with polytheistic cults is not something new. Centuries ago it intersected with paganism, and it continues to do so today. We can take a lesson from the past. The early church had to face a pagan world at every turn, and the pagans they met were not bad people. Generally, they were people looking for salvation in all the wrong places. The parallels antiquity has with Wicca and other neo-pagan cults today can teach us much.

Working on the principle that Christianity rejoices in truth wherever it may be found, the early church saw that all it had to do was redirect the focus of a certain practice or site in order for that practice or site to be used as a means of evangelization. At the birth of Christianity two thousand years ago, the missionaries went out to people who were reluctant to give up their customs and religions even as they were increasingly favorable to Christ. The Roman culture supplied a perfect set-up for this. Either people newly assumed within the empire would build a temple to a Roman god similar to one of their deities, or the Romans themselves would erect a temple to one of their gods whose attributes were similar to the gods of the peoples under them. With very few exceptions, these moves did not create any problems. The practice not only helped cement allegiance to the empire but also allowed people to hedge their bets by ensuring at least some god or goddess would hear them. Christian missionaries, in their better moments, took full advantage of this worldview with similar means.[8]

If a certain deity or festival marked something good, such as a successful catch of fish or a bountiful harvest, they would connect the blessing to Christ by calling attention to a saint whose life reflected these same qualities. For example, Saints Peter and Andrew became patrons of fishermen. On a grander scale, Mary the Mother of God replaced Cybele, Ceres, Artemis, and nearly every other goddess, for who could offer one better help, protection, warmth, and kindness than the woman who gave birth to the savior of the universe? To this day, if we were to trace the patron saints of regions, cities, towns, and professions within the oldest Christian countries and communities, more often than not, we would find at the root a pagan god or goddess. These spirits were Christianized along with the people who promulgated them.

And there is nothing wrong with that. If people then as well as today wish to be baptized into the Body of Christ, we should not be surprised if they take their whole culture with them. Of course, some things in the culture will adapt and change as a greater understanding of the Christian message takes shape, but the whole process can be seen as the way the Holy Spirit has prepared peoples across time and distance to receive the Good News of Christ. And it is ongoing.

The Tricks and Treats of Halloween

The interface between Wicca and Christianity has probably not met greater strife within certain Christian circles than Halloween, a celebration in North America whose merchandise occupies store shelves from August through October. It will not go away anytime soon, for it has as solid a Christian foundation as it does a pagan one. The upset in various church communities arises from the confusion over which feast we are celebrating every 31 October.

The Christian liturgical calendar gives us many examples of Christian adaptation of pagan practices. They are included within the discussion of Wicca, because if at one time the early Christians converted their former pagan feasts to represent the paschal mystery, today it may seem that the neo-pagan movement has taken these now-Christian feasts and recast them as pagan events. Consequently, some Christians have been left wondering whether as Christians we should be celebrating them at all, a question that is particularly troubling for the ahistorical, nonliturgical, Christian traditions.

Outlined below are dates of astronomical changes according to the solar calendar with both their Christian and pagan (usually Celtic) names.[9] There is also a brief description of how each is celebrated. Sometimes the Christians adopted and Christianized the pagan practices, and sometimes the Christian festivities were independent of them. That Christianity has anything to do with them at all, however, shows its sacramental quality.

Seasonal and Liturgical Calendar

Agrarian societies throughout history have lived their lives according to the seasons; doing so has been a matter of survival. The change of seasons and the phases of the moon marked the planting and harvesting of crops, and one had to be aware of the seasons and do everything to ensure a bountiful harvest. If the harvest failed, winter starvation was a real possibility for pagan,

Jew, and Christian alike.[10] The major hinges of the solar cycle are the spring and fall equinoxes (21 March and 21 September, respectively) and the summer and winter solstices (21 June and 21 December). The time between solstices and the equinoxes was also marked. So, halfway between 21 March and 21 June is 1 May, between 21 June and 21 September is 1 August, between 21 September and 21 December is 1 November, and between 21 December and 21 March is 1 February.

There is a major Christian feast associated with each of these calendrical markings, although with the exception of 1 November, the feasts themselves generally fall two or three days later in order not to be confused with the pagan rituals. In the cycle we see, therefore, the feast of the Annunciation (25 March), Saint Walburga (1 May),[11] the feast of Saint John the Baptist (24 June), Lammas (1 August) sometimes combined with the feast of the Tranfiguration (6 August), feast of Saint Michael and All Angels (29 September), feast of All Saints (1 November), Christmas (25 December), and the feast of the Presentation of Jesus (2 February).

On the pagan side, each of these seasonal changes entails a pagan event. What is set forth here are the modern, Wiccan names for the feasts, which may or may not reflect the names or the reasons for the ancient Celtic feasts. In fact, the origins of some of these celebrations, such as Samhein, are disputed among Wiccans today.[12] Thus, Ostara (21 March), Beltane (30 April), Litha (21 June), Lughnasadh (1 August), Mabon (21 September), Samhein (31 October), Yule (21 December), Imbolc (1 February).[13]

By far, the most controversial of all the overlaps between the Christian and Wiccan calendars is Halloween, 31 October. Certain groups of Christians are adamant that there should be no such celebration owing to its pagan background, and many school districts have banned Halloween decorations and parties. There are churches that forbid children from going out to "trick or treat." Still other churches use the opportunity to set up a "Hell House" and lead young adolescents through it in order to scare them sufficiently from engaging in sex, drugs, and rock and roll. Their concept of sin is defective, and their portrayal of Christ is nothing short of blasphemous.

The truth of Halloween, however, is not that simple. The ancient Celtic New Year, called Samhein, began on 1 November. Because a new year is always a time of change, the Celts believed that the evening before, the souls of all who died in the previous year transmigrated to the other world. In their great movement, they could stop by to visit the living and perhaps settle old scores or whatnot. The living wanted to make sure that they remained on the best of terms with the dead, so they would leave out food for them as they made their journey with hopes that the dead, now satisfied, would leave them alone. Carved, lighted turnips would either light the path for the dead or, if they had a frightening face, scare the dead away.

When he sent missionaries to England, Pope Gregory the Great instructed them not to destroy pagan shrines or forbid pagan festivals.[14] Rather, the missionaries were to redirect all pagan practices toward Christ. At first pass, it would seem that the missionaries simply substituted the Christian feast of All Saints for Samhein, but the record is not so clear about that point. The ancient Romans also had a day of the dead, celebrated on 13 May, which the early Roman Church used for All Saints, and indeed, the Roman pantheon was dedicated to Mary and all the Saints on that day in 610. From the beginning among the Greek Christians, All Saints has been celebrated the Sunday after Pentecost. The big change came in under Pope Gregory III (731–41), who moved the feast to 1 November when he dedicated an oratory to St. Peter and all apostles, martyrs, and confessors. If he had in mind the Celtic celebration of Samhein, we will never know. The fact is, however, 1 November is when All Saints has been celebrated for thirteen hundred years, and it will not go away.

The name itself, "Halloween," is a corruption of the English phrase "Hallow's Evening." It is obvious that the name incorporates the feast of All Saints. Moreover, the following day, 2 November, is the feast of All Souls, when Christians celebrate all who have died. Unlike the saints, we do not know whether or not the souls are resting in the love of Christ or are still on their journey there. For this reason, those of the catholic tradition remember them on this day and pray along with the saints that the souls will let go of their shame and guilt and move to a better place.

Every 31 October, people will celebrate Halloween, some more than others. The Wiccans will do their rituals in honor of Samhein, and the Christians will begin the All Saints celebration at sundown the evening before—or at least they will be doing something, whether or not they make the connection between the festivities of 31 October and the commemoration on 1 November. No doubt, there will be a great deal of overlap between the Wiccans and the Christians in their costumes and games, but the essential question for the Christians, regardless of the tricks and treats, is whom they ultimately see themselves following. They might not be able to respond while bobbing for apples, and it may even take a lifetime to get it exactly right, but if the answer is anywhere close to the triune God, they should simply enjoy the evening.

Summary

Neo-paganism is an outgrowth of Western culture and is expressed primarily in the movements of New Age and Wicca. New Age itself is part of Gnosticism's long legacy and exhibits the same shortcomings concerning salvation that Gnosticism did two thousand years ago. Wicca claims to date from the practices and beliefs of pre-Christian, northern Europe, but its current manifestation is closer to nineteenth- and early twentieth-century romanticism in origin. It refutes all forms of monotheism.

Wicca uses white magick to contact the spiritual world and considers it their form of prayer. It is a false comparison, however, because prayer is far different from magick. Prayer, which acknowledges God's presence in all creation, seeks to align the personal will to the will of God. White or black magick, on the other hand, works to manipulate the spirits to accomplish a human end. Through patience and mutual respect of persons, Christianity may be able to shine the light of Christ on neo-pagan movements.

The controversy over the celebration of Halloween among many Christians arises from the confusion between the commemoration of the ancient Celtic festival of Samhein and the Christian feast of All Saints. The dates of each fall at the same time. Wiccans see the occasion as Samhein and mark it accordingly, while Christians hold to All Saints and build their celebrations around that feast.

Conclusion

This discussion on the Christian interpretation of the spiritual world ends at the Feast of All Saints and All Souls, as it should. The saints, the angels, our mothers, fathers, brothers, sisters, sons, daughters, friends, and acquaintances all have the promise of sharing in the love of Christ. It is a love promised and paid for by his blood, against which Satan and the powers of darkness are absolutely powerless. The wars, violence, and injustice—the sin—we see all around us pale in the face of God's grace. With God's grace, infused into creation by Christ's incarnation, and with the prayers of the heavenly angels and saints, demons have no power; we humans on earth can fight them all. Ultimately, good always triumphs over evil.

> Christ yesterday and today
> the Beginning and the End
> the Alpha
> and the Omega
> All time belongs to him
> and all the ages
> To him be glory and power
> through every age and for ever. Amen.[1]

Christianity is not so much a fight against evil as it is a stance for good; it is a constant reminder of Christ's victory and promise. Christ's promise to us is one of blessing and eternal life with him and all our loved ones, and that eternal life begins now, in this world, even as it awaits ultimate fulfillment in the kingdom to come. With Christ and his angels at our side, we can hurry this promised kingdom through our acts of love, charity, and social justice. This promise of eternal life is really the point of our Christian existence. Saint Paul says it best:

> For the creation waits with eager longing for the revealing of the children of God; for the creation was subjected to futility, not of its own will but by the will of the one who subjected it, in hope that the creation itself will be set free from its bondage to decay and will obtain the freedom of the glory of the children of God. We know that the whole creation has been groaning in labor pains until now; and not only the creation, but we ourselves, who have the first fruits of the Spirit, groan inwardly while we wait for adoption, the redemption of our bodies. (Rom 8:19-23)

Notes

Introduction

1. From the Roman Catholic Rite of Blessing of the Easter Candle.

Chapter 1

1. The Sacred Scriptures were compiled roughly 200 BC to AD 100, when two religious movements—rabbinic Judaism and early Christianity—were taking shape and forming their own set of holy writings: the TaNaK for the Jews and the Bible containing both Old and New Testaments for the Christians. "Intertestamental" is a Christian term referring to this period.

2. I will deal more fully with the role of cherubim below.

3. That these men are angels is taken from the context of Genesis 18–19. The narrative implies in Genesis 19 that the three strangers in Genesis 18 are actually angels. The Lord God seems to speak through one of the three (Gen 18:33).

4. In the Genesis account, the sin is homosexual rape. Among the prophets and even in Jesus' preaching, the great sin is a lack of concern for social justice, adultery, dishonesty, and self-righteousness. See Isa 1:9-20; 3:9-15; Jer 23:13-14; Ezek 16:46-51; Matt 10:15; 11:24; Luke 10:12.

5. NB Lot's wife (Gen 19:17, 26); she does not heed the angel's warning.

163

6. A thorough reading of the book of Genesis will yield more instances of angels performing their beneficial functions. See Gen 21:17-20; 22:11-15; 24:7, 40; 28:12-19; 31:11; 32:1-2; 48:16.

7. More on this point below.

8. *Astarte* is the name used in 1 Samuel, 1 Kings, and 2 Kings and stems from the Babylonian pantheon, while *Astartes* is used in Judges and 1 Samuel, where, arising from Phoenician sources, she is the consort to Baal. *Asherah* appears in 1 Kings, 2 Kings, and 2 Chronicles and is similar to *Astarte*. The Hebrew uses *Ashtoreth* for both *Astarte* and *Astartes*, and biblical writers often meld the attributes of *Asherah*, *Astarte*, and *Astartes* with each other.

9. See, for example, 1 Kgs 11:1-12.

10. 1 Sam 7:3-4; 12:10.

11. Many scholars believe that this scene is the inspiration for Macbeth's visit to the "Three Weird Sisters" in William Shakespeare's *Macbeth* (IV, 1).

12. We will deal with current use of mediums and necromancy in successive chapters.

13. Note the deception of the prophet of Bethel in 1 Kings 13:11-22. The "angel" (13:18) is not really an angel.

14. "The Binding of Isaac," as the episode is formally known, has other theological interpretations as well. One is the example of Abraham's loving obedience to the Lord, where Abraham's trust in the Lord is absolute to the point that this patriarch would go so far as to let the Lord destroy his own promise to him. The other is that any one of us at any given time might be called upon to sacrifice, in a metaphorical sense, that which is most precious to us, and our only action will be to respond as Abraham responded. Finally, in the Christian Tradition, the Binding of Isaac becomes a prefiguration of Christ's choice to die on the cross as the revelation of his Father's love for creation.

15. See Lev 18:21; Deut 18:10; 2 Kgs 16:3; 17:17; 21:6; 2 Chr 28:3; 33:6; Isa 57:5; Jer 7:31; 19:5; 32:35; Ezek 16:21; 23:37.

16. Islam also differs from polytheistic faiths in this regard.

17. After the death of Solomon, the United Monarchy divides between a Northern Kingdom with a capital at Samaria and a Southern Kingdom with its capital in Jerusalem (1 Kgs 12).

18. Raphael exhorts Tobit and Tobias, "Do good and evil will not overtake you" (Tob 12:7).

Chapter 2

1. The term *satan* in Hebrew is a juridical one and literally means "adversary" or "accuser." See 1 Chr 21:1.

2. We will deal more with monolatry below.

Chapter 4

1. The name "Lucifer" is not a biblical one and enters the tradition from deuterocanonical literature and, more famously, from John Milton's great epic poem, *Paradise Lost*. We will deal with this more fully in a subsequent chapter.

2. In Luke, an angel reappears at the agony in the garden (22:43). The presence of the angels here in Matthew and Mark represents the presence of God and the divine nature of Jesus' mission.

3. "Beelzebul" at this period in Jewish history is one of the names given to the leader of the diabolical world, Satan.

4. For more on the cosmic battle, see Michael Patella, *The Death of Jesus: The Diabolical Force and the Ministering Angel, Luke 23,44-49, Cahiers de la Revue Biblique* (Paris: Gabalda, 1999).

5. In either case, the spot is on the east side of the Sea of Galilee, within the region of the pagan Decapolis, of which the cities of Gerasa and Gedara were a part.

6. Rev 3:5; 5:2, 11; 7:11; 16:5.

7. Rev 7:1-2; 8:2-13; 9:1, 11-15; 10:1, 5-10; 14:6-10, 15-18; 18:1; 20:1; 22:6-8.

8. Rev 9:15; 14:19; 15:1, 6-8; 16:2-12, 17; 17:1, 7; 18:21; 19:17.

9. Rev 19:9; 21:9, 12, 15, 17; 22:1.

10. Rev 1:20; 2:1, 8, 12, 18; 3:1, 7, 14.

11. Satan's warriors are also called "angels" in the text; this vocabulary reflects the Greek meaning that the term "angel" means "messenger," despite who is in charge.

12. Circa 164 BC.

13. Circa AD 100.

14. The terms "eschatological" and "eschatology" refer to the culmination of history, when goodness and truth will be restored in their fullness.

15. For example, Daniel (ca. 164 BC) and Joel (ca. 500–450 BC).

Chapter 5

1. While this study concentrates on Christian angelology, it also acknowledges that the other two monotheistic faiths, Judaism and Islam, also have their own understanding of these beings. Judaism, Christianity, and Islam all share the fact that angels do not compromise the uniqueness and supremacy of the one God. Other religions such as Buddhism and Hinduism have an understanding of divine beings that may have a similar function as Christian angels, but the relationship of these beings to human life, creation, and salvation are very different.

2. The Apocrypha, Deuterocanon, and Pseudepigrapha refer to the collections of works that come into existence predominantly during the intertestamental era. They feature many of the same personages of biblical canon and introduce some new ones. They derive from a number of biblical passages as well as influence biblical stories. Above all, there is no common agreement on what constitutes the various collections. The books of Tobit, Judith, First and Second Maccabees, Additions to Esther, Wisdom of Solomon, Sirach, and Additions to Daniel are for Catholics, Deuterocanonical works, but for Protestants, they are considered the Apocrypha. The Greek Church recognizes Third and Fourth Maccabees, First Esdras, and Psalm 151 as canonical, but Catholics and Protestants do not. There is more agreement on what constitutes the Pseudepigrapha, but even here, the Ethiopian Church holds Jubilees to be canonical.

3. The Donation of Constantine was a forged document used to support the papal claim that Emperor Constantine gave the Western Empire to the Pope. The document itself, as Valla showed, dates from approximately AD 900.

4. Pope Greogry alludes to a variation in the hierarchy rather than specifies one. See *Moralia in Job* (XXXIII, xx, 37) [Latin and French; introduction and notes by Adalbert de Vogüé; translation by Benedictine Nuns of Wisques (Sources chrétiennes, 538. Paris: Cerf, 2010) 115].

5. Gregory the Great moves the Principalities up to the second tier and the Virtues down to the third. Saint Bernard follows Gregory's ranking, but Dante holds to one promoted by Pseudo-Dionysius. See Joad Raymond, *Milton's Angels* (New York: Oxford University Press, 2010), 24.

6. See Michael Patella, *Lord of the Cosmos: Mithras, Paul, and the Gospel of Mark* (New York: T & T Clark, 2006).

7. Ezek 10; 11:22; 41:18-25.

8. "Virtues" and "Principalities" are sometimes read as "rulers" or "authorities." In addition, early church fathers do not always agree on the list of angels. In time, Pseudo-Dionysius' arrangement holds sway.

9. See David Keck, *Angels and Angelology in the Middle Ages* (New York: Oxford University Press, 1998), 11–70.

10. Ibid., 62.

11. It is easy to confuse depictions of Saint Michael with those of Saint George. Saint George, who is not an angel, is shown slaying a dragon.

12. See Keck, *Angels and Angelology*, 161–88.

13. A personal spirit for the Greeks was called a *daimon*. See ibid., 161.

14. There are certainly factors that can hinder free will, such as emotional and physical exhaustion, trauma, substance abuse, lack of knowledge, psychological issues, etc., but all things being equal, each human being has free will, which no power can alter.

Chapter 6

1. See David Keck, *Angels and Angelology in the Middle Ages* (New York: Oxford University Press, 1998), 165–70.

2. See ibid., 170–71.

3. Mark 16:1-8 and Luke 24:1-10 mention "man" and "two men" respectively.

4. Judaism as well as Islam also believes that creation is sacred. Christianity's difference is that because of the incarnation the whole universe is saved and nothing within it is to be considered unclean or prohibited. This understanding is also the reason why Christianity allows for images and statues, for if God puts on the elements of creation, the elements of creation can reflect the glory of God.

5. See Matt 7:21-23; 25:31-46; and especially Matt 14:15-21; 15:32-39; Mark 6:34-44; 8:1-9; Luke 9:12-17; John 6:5-14 where care of the spirit (preaching) and care of the body (feeding) are paired.

6. "Eschatology" refers to the last days of the universe or the end of the world.

Chapter 7

1. Stoicism is a Greek philosophy based broadly on the writings of Plato, which maintained a definite split between the physical and spiritual life. For Platonists and Stoics, the spiritual is pure and good.

2. In Buddhist thought, a totally selfless person could opt to become a Bodhisattva, or "enlightened being" who will suffer for the sake of any other living, sentient being, even if it means descending to a lower form of life. From a Buddhist perspective, therefore, Jesus Christ would be a Bodhisattva.

3. Acts, Romans, Galatians, 1 Timothy, Titus, 1 John, and Jude. There is also one reference in 4 Maccabees, held by the Greek Church to be deuterocanonical.

4. See Matt 28:1-20; Mark 16:1-20; Luke 24:1-53; John 20:1-21, 25.

5. Contemplation on these mysteries is the material of the great Christian mystics such as Gregory the Illuminator, Julian of Norwich, John of the Cross, and Theresa of Avila.

6. See Matt 17:1-9; Mark 9:1-9; Luke 9:28-36.

7. Elisabeth Kubler-Ross, *On Death and Dying* (New York: Simon & Schuster, Touchstone Book, 1997).

8. Charles Dickens, *A Christmas Carol* (New York: Stewart, Tabori, and Chang, 1990).

9. Ross, *Death.*

10. C. S. Lewis, *The Great Divorce* (New York: Macmillan, 1946).

11. Lewis draws on the medieval notion of a *refrigerium* or holiday obtained for the souls of the damned by the prayers of the Blessed Mother and the saints.

12. Lewis, *The Great Divorce*, 8.

13. Ibid., 9.

14. Napoleon is speaking about his own generals whom he feels betrayed him, his own wife who was unfaithful to him, and the nations who defeated him (ibid., 11).

15. Ultimately, of course, Napoleon is only an example for the plot. Neither Lewis nor we know whether or not Napoleon (or Hitler, Stalin, Pol Pot, or anyone we might consider a monstrous criminal) is in hell. Whereas the church has always taught the existence of hell, the church has always refused to state who is there. God alone can read the human heart, and God alone knows what has happened to people whom history has condemned.

16. The icon on the cover of this book entitled, "Saint Michael contending with the Devil over the soul of a rich man," visually renders the same lesson.

17. We will take up the topic of the condemned and hell below.

18. Eccl 11:1; Hos 8:7; Matt 7:1-2; Mark 4:24-25; Luke 6:37-38.

19. The communion of saints is comprised of angels and the deceased in heaven in concert with those on earth. See below.

20. Beatrice represents love and redemption. Dante Alighieri, *Purgatorio*, trans., Jean Hollander and Robert Hollander (New York: Doubleday, 2003).

21. John Henry Cardinal Newman, *The Dream of Gerontius* (New York: Longmans, Green, and Co., 1915), 66.

22. See Matt 13:36-43; 16:24-28; 24:30-31; 25:31; Mark 8:38; 13:26-27; Luke 15:10; 16:22.

23. Craig Callender, "Is Time an Illusion?," *Scientific American* (May 24, 2010).

24. John Donne, Meditation 17, in *Devotions upon Emergent Occasions* (Ann Arbor: University of Michigan Press, 1959), 107–9. The reader is asked to remember that the gender exclusive language is historically bound in the culture of seventeenth-century England.

25. See also Mark 13:32.

26. The Roman Catholic Church has had a formal process to elevate someone to sainthood, called "canonization," since at least the thirteenth century; this process has been revised through the centuries, most recently under Pope John Paul II in 1983.

27. Matt 22:1-22; Luke 14:15-24; and also Matt 14:15-21; 15:32-39; Mark 6:37-44; 8:1-9; Luke 9:13-17; John 6:5-14. See also Isa 25:6.

Chapter 8

1. Genesis has two main sections. The "Mythological History" (Gen 1–11:25) deals with the great questions of human existence, such as the reasons for creation, suffering, pain, sin, and even love. The "Legendary History" (Gen 11:26–50:26) relates the history of real people in real time which may have factual inaccuracies.

2. Grant McColley, *Paradise Lost: An Account of Its Growth and Major Origins, with a Discussion of Milton's Use of Sources and Literary Patterns* (Chicago: Packard and Company, 1940), 3.

3. Ibid., 4.

4. Ibid., 10.

5. Ibid., 11.

6. While the tradition at various points refers to Lucifer as the "highest" angel, perhaps even one of the cherubim, most often he is depicted as a fallen archangel and, therefore, Saint Michael's antithesis. Related more so on the level of human experience than literary borrowing is the Greek term, *daimon*, from which we get our word "demon." *Daimon* originally was a lesser god. Socrates, for example, speaks about a personal *daimon* in such a way that it seems very similar to the Christian description of a guardian angel. Within the thought of the hexameral tradition, it is easy to see how a *daimon* would follow the example of Lucifer and become a "demon."

7. Note here the obvious references to Rev 12, a chapter that undoubtedly influenced Milton as he penned this section of *Paradise Lost*.

8. Zoroastrianism is more complex in its tenets than this very brief explanation can offer, and a full treatment of the religion is beyond the scope of this primer. For more on Zoroastrianism, see Mary Boyce, *A History of Zoroastrianism* (New York: E. J. Brill, 1996).

9. For example, see Mozart's *Don Giovanni* and Charles Gounod's *Faust*.

10. A sacramental life will inevitably gravitate toward the material and concrete, even in metaphysical descriptions. The use of metaphor in Christian literature and life always surfaces somehow, especially in Catholicism.

11. One can even say that this situation exists today. Moloch, Pazazu, Baal, Pan, not to mention nameless satyrs, are all names for or manifestations of Satan.

12. Matt 12:24-28; Mark 3:22-27; Luke 11:14-20.

Chapter 9

1. Tim Vivian, trans., *Four Desert Fathers: Pambo, Evagrius, Macarius of Egypt, and Macarius of Alexandria* (Crestwood, NY: Saint Vladimir's Seminary Press, 2004), 75–78.

2. Ibid., 75.

3. Ibid., 106-8.

4. We should recall here how we meet angels and all things good in the sacramental life.

Chapter 10

1. Practices which seek to contact the dead.

2. In Christianity, the spiritual world is mysterious, not secret, the difference being that access to the mysterious world is open to all, even though full understanding of the mystery may never be accessible in this life. Moreover, Christian mystery is oriented toward all that is true, good, and beautiful in the one God. A *secret* spiritual world, on the other hand, is closed to all but a group of experts who profess to have knowledge unavailable to others. In addition, it is geared toward manipulation of spirits.

3. Spiritualism certainly had its antecedents, and to trace its origins is nearly impossible, but with the Fox sisters it garnered tremendous excitement and popularity in the antebellum United States (Robert S. Cox, *Body and Soul and Sympathetic History of American Spiritualism* [Charlottesville: University of Virginia Press, 2003], 5–6).

4. Barbara Weisberg, *Talking to the Dead: Kate and Maggie Fox and the Rise of Spiritualism* (San Francisco: HarperSanFrancisco, 2004), 241–45.

5. Anton Szandor LaVey, *The Satanic Bible* (New York: Avon Books, 1969).

Chapter 11

1. "Infestation," "oppression," "obsession," and "possession" are terms used by the International Association of Exorcists (Matt Baglio, *The Rite: The Making of a Modern Exorcist* [New York: Doubleday, 2009], 47–50).

2. Ibid., 48.

3. Athanasius of Alexandria, *The Life of Antony: The Coptic Life and the Greek Life*, trans. Tim Vivian and Apostolos N. Athanassakis with Roman Greer (Kalamazoo, MI: Cistercian Publications, 2003), 79.

4. Personal communication, Angela G. Del Greco, hermit and spiritual director.

5. Mark 1:23-26; 7:25-30; 9:17-27; Luke 4:33-35; 9:38-42. In the gospels, "unclean spirit" and "demon" are used interchangeably.

6. Matt 9:32-33; 15:22-28; Mark 7:25-30; Luke 11:14.

7. Matt 4:1-11; 13:36-43; Mark 1:13; 3:22-27; Luke 4:1-13; 13:11-16; 22:3; John 13:37. In the gospels, "Satan," "devil," and "Beelzebul" are used interchangeably.

8. Material for this section has been adapted from *Roman Ritual for Exorcism*, 1998, as well as Gabriele Amorth, *An Exorcist, More Stories* (San Francisco: Ignatius Press, 2002), 78–82.

9. A possessed person alternates between periods of quiet, if not normalcy, and periods of *crisis* during which the demons manifest themselves. At these times, the victim is in a trance-like state, and the unclean spirit takes over all physical activity. Generally, when the victim is no longer in crisis, the exorcist or anyone else can have a near-normal conversation with the victim, though signs of agitation can still be present.

10. Amorth, *An Exorcist*, 114–15.

11. In the German legend, Faustus sells his soul to the devil in return for unlimited knowledge. The story has become the basis for Christopher Marlowe's play; Johann Wolfgang von Goethe's great poem; the operas of Charles Gounod, Arrigo Boito, and Ferruccio Busoni; musical works of Hector Berlioz, Gustav Mahler, Franz Liszt, Robert Schumann, and Havergal Brian; and even the Broadway musical, *Damn Yankees*.

12. See the works of Amorth and Baglio.

Chapter 12

1. Christianity believes, of course, that there are three persons in one God: Father, Son, and Holy Spirit.

2. See A Fellow of the Theosophical Society, *What Is Theosophy?* (Boston: Cupples, Upham, and Company, 1886); Alice A. Bailey, *From Bethlehem to Calvary* (New York: Lucis Publishing Company, 1937).

3. Raymond Buckland in *The Witch Book: The Encyclopedia of Witchcraft, Wicca, and New-Paganisms* (Detroit: Visible Ink Press, 2002) relies on the famous occultist, A. E. Waite (1857–1942), who links Wicca with pre-Christian traditions. Other scholars have since demonstrated that the connection between what exists in Wicca today and what the ancients believed is tenuous at best.

4. Robin Briggs, *Witches and Neighbors* (New York: Viking Penguin, 1996).

5. Margaret Alice Murray, *The Witch-Cult in Western Europe* (Oxford: Clarendon Press, 1962; originally printed 1921).

6. Buckland, *The Witch Book*.

7. Norman Cohn, *Europe's Inner Demons* (New York: New American Library, 1975). Rev. edition: *Europe's Inner Demons: The Demonization of Christians in Medieval Christendom* (Chicago: University of Chicago Press, 2000); Keith Thomas, *Religion and the Decline of Magic: Studies in Popular Beliefs in Sixteenth and Seventeenth Century England* (London: Weidenfeld & Nicolson, 1997); Ronald Hutton, *The Pagan Religions of the Ancient British Isles: Their Nature and Legacy* (Cambridge, MA: Blackwell, 1991); *The Triumph of the Moon* (New York: Oxford University Press, 1999).

8. Missionaries in their worst moments, however, burned and destroyed the pagan temples and holy sites. For this and other crimes committed in the church's name, Pope John Paul II publically apologized on 12 March 2000 as part of the commemoration of Christianity's third millennium.

9. Buckland, *The Witch Book*.

10. The seasons are not the only influence on the Christian liturgical calendar. Saints' feast days generally fall on the anniversary of death or martyrdom.

11. Saint Walburga was a Christian missionary to England whose cult was very popular in the Middle Ages. The Christian liturgical calendar no longer has a major celebration for Saint Walburga's feast, though May Day is an important holiday for the labor movement in Europe. It seems that Christian Easter and Pentecost, which occur on either side of 1 May, have replaced the saint's feast as a holy day celebration, but this assumption needs more study.

12. See Hutton, *The Pagan Religions of the Ancient British Isles*.

13. Buckland, *The Witch Book*.

14. Epistle XI, 156, as cited in R. A. Markus, *Gregory Great and His World* (Edinburgh: Cambridge University Press, 1997), 183.

Conclusion

1. From the Roman Catholic Rite of Blessing of the Easter Candle.

Bibliography

A Fellow of the Theosophical Society. *What Is Theosophy?* Boston: Cupples, Upham, and Company, 1886.

Amorth, Gabriele. *An Exorcist, More Stories.* San Francisco: Ignatius Press, 2002.

———. *An Exorcist Tells His Story.* San Francisco: Ignatius Press, 1999.

Athanasius of Alexandria. *The Life of Antony: The Coptic Life and the Greek Life.* Translated by Tim Vivian and Apostolos N. Athanassakis with Roman Greer. Kalamazoo, MI: Cistercian Publications, 2003.

Baglio, Matt. *The Rite: The Making of a Modern Exorcist.* New York: Doubleday, 2009.

Bailey, Alice A. *From Bethlehem to Calvary.* New York: Lucis Publishing Company, 1937.

Boyce, Mary. *A History of Zoroastrianism.* New York: E. J. Brill, 1996.

Briggs, Robin. *Witches and Neighbors.* New York: Viking Penguin, 1996.

Buckland, Raymond. *The Witch Book: The Encyclopedia of Witchcraft, Wicca, and New-Paganisms.* Detroit: Visible Ink Press, 2002.

Callender, Craig. "Is Time an Illusion?" *Scientific American* (May 24, 2010).

Cohn, Norman. *Europe's Inner Demons.* New York: New American Library, 1975. Rev. edition: *Europe's Inner Demons: The Demonization of Christians in Medieval Christendom.* Chicago: University of Chicago Press, 2000.

Cox, Robert S. *Body and Soul and Sympathetic History of American Spiritualism.* Charlottesville: University of Virginia Press, 2003.

Dickens, Charles. *A Christmas Carol.* New York: Stewart, Tabori, and Chang, 1990.

Donne, John. *Devotions upon Emergent Occasions.* Ann Arbor: University of Michigan Press, 1959.

Gregory I, Pope. *Moralia in Job.* Latin and French. Introduction and notes by Adalbert de Vogüé. Translated by Benedictine Nuns of Wisques. Sources chrétiennes 538. Paris: Cerf, 2010.

Hutton, Ronald. *The Pagan Religions of the Ancient British Isles: Their Nature and Legacy.* Cambridge, MA: Blackwell, 1991.

———. *The Triumph of the Moon.* New York: Oxford University Press, 1999.

Keck, David. *Angels and Angelology in the Middle Ages.* New York: Oxford University Press, 1998.

Kubler-Ross, Elisabeth. *On Death and Dying.* New York, NY: Simon & Schuster, Touchstone Book, 1997.

LaVey, Anton Szandor. *The Satanic Bible.* New York: Avon Books, 1969.

Lewis, C. S. *The Great Divorce.* New York: Macmillan Company, 1946.

Markus, R. A. *Gregory Great and His World.* Edinburgh: Cambridge University Press, 1997.

McColley, Grant. *Paradise Lost: An Account of Its Growth and Major Origins, with a Discussion of Milton's Use of Sources and Literary Patterns.* Chicago: Packard and Company, 1940.

Murray, Margaret Alice. *The Witch-Cult in Western Europe.* Oxford: Clarendon Press, 1962; originally printed 1921.

Newman, John Henry Cardinal. *The Dream of Gerontius*. New York: Longmans, Green, and Company, 1915.

Patella, Michael. *The Death of Jesus: The Diabolical Force and the Ministering Angel, Luke 23,44-49. Cahiers de la Revue Biblique* 43. Paris: Gabalda, 1999.

―――. *Lord of the Cosmos: Mithras, Paul, and the Gospel of Mark*. New York: T & T Clark, 2006.

Raymond, Joad. *Milton's Angels, the Early-Modern Imagination*. New York: Oxford University Press, 2010.

Roman Ritual for Exorcism, 1998.

Thomas, Keith. *Religion and the Decline of Magic: Studies in Popular Beliefs in Sixteenth and Seventeenth Century England*. London: Weidenfeld & Nicolson, 1997.

Vivian, Tim, trans. *Four Desert Fathers: Pambo, Evagrius, Macarius of Egypt, and Macarius of Alexandria*. Crestwood, NY: Saint Vladimir's Seminary Press, 2004.

Weisberg, Barbara. *Talking to the Dead: Kate and Maggie Fox and the Rise of Spiritualism*. San Francisco: HarperSanFrancisco, 2004.

Further Reading

Barker, Margaret. *The Great Angel.* Louisville: Westminster/John Knox Press, 1992.

Barton, Blanche. *The Secret Life of a Satanist: The Authorized Biography of Anton LaVey.* Los Angeles, CA: Feral House, 1990.

Bell, Richard H. *Deliver Us from Evil: Interpreting the Redemption from the Power of Satan in New Testament Theology.* Wissenschaftliche Untersuchungen zum Neuen, Testament 216. Tübingen: Mohr Siebeck, 2007.

Chase, Steven, trans. *Angelic Spirituality.* New York: Paulist Press, 2002.

Donne, John. *Death's Duel.* Ann Arbor: The University of Michigan Press, 1959.

Ellis, Bill. *Raising the Devil: Satanism, New Religions, and the Media.* Lexington: University Press of Kentucky, 2000.

Frankfurter, David. *Evil Incarnate, Rumors of Demonic Conspiracy and Satanic Abuse in History.* Princeton, NJ: Princeton University Press, 2006.

Fredriksen, Paula. *From Jesus to Christ: The Origins of the New Testament Images of Christ.* New Haven, CT: Yale University Press, 2000.

Gieschen, Charles. *Angelmorphic Christology.* Boston: Brill, 1998.

Hannah, Darrell D. *Michael and Christ: Michael Traditions and Angel Christology in Early Christianity.* Tübingen: J. C. B. Mohr (Paul Siebeck), 1999.

Kerr, Howard. *Mediums, and Spirit-Rappers, and Roaring Radicals: Spiritualism in American Literature, 1850–1900.* Urbana: University of Illinois Press, 1972.

Kreeft, Peter. *Angels (and Demons) and What Do We Really Know about Them?* San Francisco: Ignatius Press, 1995.

Luibheid, Colm, trans. *Pseudo-Dionysius: The Complete Works.* Classics of Western Spirituality. New York: Paulist Press, 1987.

Rodewyk, Adolf. *Possessed by Satan: The Church's Teaching on the Devil, Possession, and Exorcism.* Translated by Martin Ebon. New York: Doubleday and Company, 1975.

Stuart, Nancy Rubin. *The Reluctant Spiritualist: The Life of Maggie Fox.* New York: Harcourt, 2005.

Vogl, Carl. *Begone, Satan!* Translated by Celestine Kapsner. Rockford, IL: Tan Books, 1973.

Scripture Index

Genesis

Book of	3–5, 53
1–11:25	170n1
1:1–2:3	47
3	4
3:1-8	3
3:14-15	47
4:7	4
6:1-5	108
6:4	60, 109
11:26–50:26	170n1
15:1-21	12
16:7	5
17:1-15	12
18–19	5, 163n3
18:10	5
18:33	163n3
19:1-22	5
19:17	163n5
19:26	163n5
21:17-20	164n6
22:1-18	11, 164n14
22:11-15	164n6
24:7	164n6
24:40	164n6
28:12-19	164n6
31:11	164n6
32:1-2	164n6
48:16	164n6

Exodus

Book of	5–6, 65
3:2	6
3:4	6
3:4-15	12
3:14	151
13:21	6
14:19	6
14:24	6
19–20	12
20:4	151

Leviticus

Book of	6–7
18:21	164n15
19:31	10
20:27	10

Numbers
Book of   6–7

Deuteronomy
Book of   6–7
4   6
12   6
13   6
18:10   164n15
18:10-13   11

Joshua
5:13–6:5   7

Judges
Book of   164n8
2:1-3   7
6:25-31   8
13–16   9
13:6   9
13:18-20   9

1 Samuel
Book of   53, 164n8
7:3-4   164n10
12:10   164n10
13:18-20   9
15   10
28:8-25   10
28:9   10
28:12   10

2 Samuel
Book of   9

1 Kings
Book of   53, 65, 164n8

1–16   10
11:1   11
11:1-12   164n9
11:2-10   11
11:7-8   11
12   164n17
13:11-22   164n13
13:18   164n13
16:31   13
17–19   10
18   13
18:1-2   14
18:19   13
18:26   13, 14
18:28-29   13
18:30-35   14
18:36   14
20–22   10

2 Kings
Book of   164n8
1:16   14
5:1-15   14
16:1-5   26
16:3   164n15
17:17   164n15
21:6   164n15

1 Chronicles
Book of   65
21:1   165n2

2 Chronicles
Book of   65, 164n8
28:3   164n15
33:6   164n15

Tobit

Book of	53, 68, 166n2
3:16-17	15
5:17	69
6	15
6:1	15
7:9-16	15
8:1-8	15
11	68
11:4	15
12:7	165n1
12:12	16
12:14	16
12:15	16(2), 61
14:4	16
14:6	16

Judith

Book of	166n2

Esther

Additions to	166n2

1 Maccabees

Book of	166n2

2 Maccabees

Book of	166n2

Psalms

Book of	53
16	19
18:10	65
58	19
80:1-2	65
82	19
84	19
86	19
96	19
97	19
106	19
106:28	20
106:37	20
115:1-7	116
135	19
135:5-7	116
136	19

Job

Book of	53
1:6-12	19

Proverbs

Book of	53
1:7	20
2:13-14	20
4:18	21
4:26	21
24:9	20

Ecclesiastes

11:1	169n18

Wisdom

Book of	53, 166n2
1:12-15	21
1:16	21
2:1-11	21
2:12	21
2:12-20	21
2:20	21
2:24	22
3:1-9	22
5:13	22

5:15-20	22
11:15	22
12:3-6	22
13–15	22
14:23-26	22
15:1-3	22

Sirach

Book of	166n2
1:22-30	23
34	23
34:5	24
34:6-7	24

Isaiah

1:9-20	163n4
3:9-15	163n4
6:2	64
6:2-3	64
6:3	75
6:6	64
7	26
7:13-14	26
14:11-15	107
25:6	169n27
45–46	26
45:9-12	27
45:20-25	27
57–59	27
57:1-10	27
57:5	164n15
57:11-13	27
58:3-7	27
58:13-14	27
60–61	27
65:17-25	27

Jeremiah

7:31	164n15
19:5	164n15
23:13-14	163n4
32:35	164n15

Ezekiel

Book of	65
10	167n7
11:22	167n7
16:21	164n15
16:46-51	163n4
23:37	164n15
41:18-25	167n7

Daniel

Additions to	166n2
Book of	43, 166n15
8:16	68
9:21	68
10:13	61, 67
10:21	61, 67
12:1	61, 67

Hosea

8:7	169n18

Joel

Book of	166n15

Matthew

Gospel of	29, 49, 82
1:20-24	71
2:13	72
2:19	72
4:1-11	30, 172n7
7:1-2	41, 169n18

7:21-23	168n5
8:28	33
8:28-34	33
9:32-33	172n6
10:15	163n4
11:24	163n4
12:22-32	32
12:24-28	170n12
13:24-30	49
13:36-43	49, 169n22, 172n6
14:15-21	168n5, 169n27
15:22-28	172n6
15:32-39	168n5, 169n27
16:24-28	169n22
17:1-9	168n6
17:14-18	137
17:15	137
18:10	69
22:1-22	169n27
24:3-44	41, 49
24:29	50
24:30-31	169n22
24:36	50, 97
25:31	169n22
25:31-46	41, 50, 89, 168n5
25:37	51
27:51-54	51
28:1-7	72
28:1-20	168n4
28:2	51

Mark

Gospel of	29, 49, 82, 167n6
1:12	30

1:12-13	30
1:13	172n7
1:23-26	172n5
3:22-27	170n12, 172n7
3:22-30	32
4:24-25	169n18
5:1-20	33
5:9	143
5:10	34
6:34-44	168n5
6:37-44	169n27
7:25-30	172n5, 172n6
8:1-9	168n5, 169n27
8:38	169n22
9:1-9	168n6
9:17-27	172n5
9:21-25	137
9:28-29	142
13:1-37	41
13:14	50
13:26-27	169n22
13:32	50, 169n25
16:1-8	167n3
16:1-20	168n4

Luke

Gospel of	29, 49, 82
1:11-20	68
1:19	61, 72
1:26	61
1:26-38	68, 72
1:28-31	72
2:14	75
4:1-13	30, 172n7
4:16-19	140
4:33-35	172n5
6:37-38	41, 169n18

8:26-39	33	8:32	92
8:28	33(2)	13:37	172n7
8:29	33	20:1-21	168n4
8:30	143	20:11-15	72
8:31	34, 145	20:25	168n4
9:13-17	169n27		
9:28-36	168n6	**Acts**	
9:38-42	172n5	Book of	62, 82, 168n3
10:12	163n4	12:14-15	69
11:14	172n6	16:16-18	141
11:14-20	170n12	17:18-34	62
11:14-23	32		
11:24-26	144	**Romans**	
13:1-13	137	Letter	35, 168n3
13:10-16	137	8:19-21	98
13:11	137	8:19-23	162
13:11-16	172n7	8:38	65
14:15-24	169n27		
15:10	169n22	**1 Corinthians**	
16:19-31	89	Letter	35
16:22	169n22	8:4	35
16:24	89	10:14-29	35, 36
16:26	89	10:26	26, 36
21:6-36	41		
22:3	172n7	**2 Corinthians**	
22:43	165n2	Letter	35
23:44-49	165n4		
24:1-10	167n3	**Galatians**	
24:1-53	168n4	Letter	35, 168n3
24:39-43	82–83		
		Ephesians	
John		Letter	35
Gospel of	29, 82	1:21	65
1:29	75	3:10	65
1:36	75		
3:17	52	**Philippians**	
6:5-14	168n5, 169n27	Letter	35

Colossians

Letter	35
1:16	65
2:8	134
2:8-16	37
2:10	65
2:16-20	35, 37
2:17-20	37
2:20	38

1 Thessalonians

Letter	35, 41
4:14-18	39, 40
4:16	67

2 Thessalonians

Letter	35

1 Timothy

Letter	35, 168n3

2 Timothy

Letter	35

Titus

Letter	35, 168n3

Philemon

Letter	35

Hebrews

1:1-3	154

1 John

Letter	168n3
4:1	24

Jude

Letter	168n3
1:9	61, 67

Revelation

Book of	41, 43, 44, 54
1:1	42
1:1b	42
1:20	165n10
2:1	165n10
2:8	165n10
2:12	165n10
2:18	165n10
3:1	165n10
3:5	165n6
3:7	165n10
3:14	165n10
4:8	75
5:2	165n6
5:6	75
5:11	165n6
5:11-12	75
5:12	75
7:1-2	165n7
7:9	45
7:11	165n6
8:2-13	165n7
9:1	165n7
9:15	165n8
10:1	165n7
10:5-10	165n7
11	46
11–15	165n7
11–20	44
11:3	47(2)
11:7	44
11:13	45

11:15	46
11:17-19	45
12	44, 45, 170n7
12–13	48
12:1-2	46
12:4-5	47
12:5	47
12:6	47
12:7	42, 61, 68
12:9	42, 44
12:13-17	47
12:16	47
13:1	44
13:1-10	44
13:2	44
13:4	44
13:8	75
13:11-18	44
13:18	44
14:1	45
14:6-10	165n7
14:15-18	165n7
14:19	165n8
15:1	42, 165n8
15:6-8	165n8
16:2-12	165n8
16:5	165n6
16:17	165n8
17:1	165n8
17:7	165n8
18:1	165n7
18:21	42, 165n8
19:9	42, 165n9
19:17	165n8
20:1	165n7
21–22	52

21:3	52
21:9	42, 165n9
21:12	165n9
21:15	165n9
21:17	165n9
21:24-27	74
22:1	165n9
22:6-8	165n7
22:8-9	42
22:16	42(2)
22:17	55

1 Esdras
Book of	166n2

Psalm 151
	166n2

3 Maccabees
Book of	166n2

4 Esdras
Book of	67

4 Maccabees
Book of	166n2, 168n3

1 Enoch
Book of	60

2 Enoch
Book of	60

Jubilees
Book of	166n2